United States Government Accountability Office

A Report to Congressional Requesters

I0415896

September 2012

BUREAU OF PRISONS

Growing Inmate Crowding Negatively Affects Inmates, Staff, and Infrastructure

G A O

Accountability ★ Integrity ★ Reliability

GAO-12-743

September 2012

G A O
Accountability * Integrity * Reliability

Highlights

Highlights of GAO-12-743, a report to congressional requesters

BUREAU OF PRISONS

Growing Inmate Crowding Negatively Affects Inmates, Staff, and Infrastructure

Why GAO Did This Study

BOP operates 117 federal prisons to house approximately 178,000 federal offenders, and contracts with private companies and some state governments to house about another 40,000 inmates. BOP calculates the number of prisoners that each BOP-run institution can house safely and securely (i.e., rated capacity). GAO was asked to address (1) the growth in BOP's population from fiscal years 2006 through 2011 and BOP's projections for inmate population and capacity; (2) the effects of a growing federal prison population on operations within BOP facilities, and the extent to which BOP has taken actions to mitigate these effects; and (3) actions selected states have taken to reduce their prison populations, and the extent to which BOP has implemented similar initiatives.

GAO analyzed BOP's inmate population data from fiscal years 2006 through 2011, BOP's 2020 long-range capacity plan, and BOP policies and statutory authority. GAO visited five federal prisons chosen on the basis of geographic dispersion and varying security levels. The results are not generalizable, but provide information on the effects of a growing prison population. GAO selected five states based on actions they took to mitigate the effects of their growing prison populations—and assessed the extent to which their actions would be possible for BOP. GAO makes no recommendations in this report. BOP provided technical clarifications, which GAO incorporated where appropriate.

View GAO-12-743. For more information, contact David C. Maurer at (202) 512-9627 or maurerd@gao.gov.

What GAO Found

The Department of Justice's Bureau of Prisons' (BOP) 9.5 percent population growth from fiscal years 2006 through 2011 exceeded the 7 percent increase in its rated capacity, and BOP projects continued population growth. Growth was most concentrated among male inmates, and in 2011, 48 percent of the inmates BOP housed were sentenced for drugs. From fiscal years 2006 through 2011, BOP increased its rated capacity by about 8,300 beds as a result of opening 5 new facilities and closing 4 minimum security camps, but because of the population expansion, crowding (or population in excess of rated capacity) increased from 36 to 39 percent. In 2011 crowding was most severe (55 percent) in highest security facilities. BOP's 2020 long-range capacity plan projects continued growth in the federal prison population from fiscal years 2012 through 2020, with systemwide crowding exceeding 45 percent through 2018.

According to BOP, the growth in the federal inmate population has negatively affected inmates, staff, and infrastructure, but BOP has acted within its authority to help mitigate the effects of this growth. BOP officials reported increased use of double and triple bunking, waiting lists for education and drug treatment programs, limited meaningful work opportunities, and increased inmate-to-staff ratios. These factors, taken together, contribute to increased inmate misconduct, which negatively affects the safety and security of inmates and staff. BOP officials and union representatives voiced concerns about a serious incident occurring. To manage its growing population, BOP staggers meal times and segregates inmates involved in disciplinary infractions, among other things.

The five states in GAO's review have taken more actions than BOP to reduce their prison populations, because these states have legislative authority that BOP does not have. These states have modified criminal statutes and sentencing, relocated inmates to local facilities, and provided inmates with additional opportunities for early release. BOP generally does not have similar authority. For example, BOP cannot shorten an inmate's sentence or transfer inmates to local prisons. Efforts to address the crowding issue could include (1) reducing the inmate population by actions such as reforming sentencing laws, (2) increasing capacity by actions such as constructing new prisons, or (3) some combination of both.

A Triple-Bunked Cell in a BOP Facility

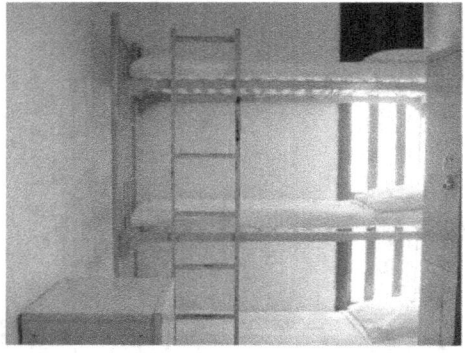

Source: BOP.

_____ United States Government Accountability Office

Contents

Figures

Abbreviations

ACA	American Correctional Association
ADP	average daily population
ADX	Administrative Maximum
BOP	Bureau of Prisons
DHO	disciplinary hearing officer
DOJ	Department of Justice
ESL	English as a Second Language
GED	General Educational Development
IG	Inspector General
NIC	National Institute of Corrections
OMB	Office of Management and Budget
PHS	Public Health Service
RDAP	Residential Drug Abuse Program
RICO	Racketeer Influenced and Corrupt Organizations Act
RRC	Residential Reentry Center
S&E	Salaries and Expenses
UDC	Unit Discipline Committee

United States Government Accountability Office
Washington, DC 20548

September 12, 2012

The Honorable Elijah E. Cummings
Ranking Member
Committee on Oversight
    and Government Reform
House of Representatives

The Honorable Robert C. Scott
Ranking Member
Subcommittee on Crime, Terrorism,
    and Homeland Security
Committee on the Judiciary
House of Representatives

As of December 2010, federal and state correctional facilities incarcerated more than 1.6 million persons (about 1 in 200 U.S. residents), according to the most recently available data from the U.S. Department of Justice (DOJ).[1] At the federal level, DOJ's Bureau of Prisons (BOP) is responsible for approximately 218,000 of these inmates, with a fiscal year 2012 operating budget of about $6.6 billion—the second largest budget within DOJ.[2] BOP's population has increased by more than 400 percent since the late 1980s, and by about 50 percent since 2000. According to BOP, this growth is primarily attributed to an increase in inmates' sentence length over time.[3] At the end of fiscal year 2011, BOP housed nearly 178,000 inmates in the 117 institutions that it owns

---

[1]See Department of Justice, Bureau of Justice Statistics, *Prisoners in 2010* (Washington, D.C.: December 2011). The Bureau of Justice Statistics is the statistical agency of DOJ.

[2]The Federal Bureau of Investigation has the largest budget within DOJ at $8 billion. BOP's $6.6 billion includes $6.551 billion for salaries and expenses and $90 million for buildings and facilities.

[3]The Sentencing Reform Act of 1984, Pub. L. No 98-473, 98 Stat. 1987, changed the federal sentencing structure. The act was effective for offenses committed on or after November 1, 1987. The act abolished parole, and subsequent legislation established mandatory minimum sentences for many federal offenses, which limits the authority that BOP has to affect the length of the sentence or the size of the inmate population.

GAO-12-743 Federal Prison Crowding

and operates, and it contracted with other correctional facilities, such as those of states and private companies, to house nearly 40,000 inmates.[4]

BOP calculates the number of prisoners a given prison facility is built to house safely and securely and calls this its rated capacity.[5] Crowding, as defined by BOP, is the extent to which a facility's inmate population level exceeds its rated capacity.[6] Systemwide, BOP prisons exceed their rated capacity by 39 percent, and crowding has been a significant ongoing concern. Assessments conducted through the Federal Managers' Financial Integrity Act have identified prison crowding as a material weakness since 2006.[7] Further, since that same year, DOJ's Inspector General (IG) has included detention and incarceration among DOJ's top 10 management and performance challenges departmentwide. In its 2011 list of challenges, the IG noted its concerns regarding the impact of federal prison crowding and the related stresses on BOP's prison staffing regarding BOP's ability to safely manage the increasing federal inmate population.[8] The Attorney General has reported both of these findings annually in his performance and accountability report for the department.

While federal inmate population growth has been steady, the overall growth of the state inmate population began to decline in 2009. DOJ reports that the overall state prison population increased from calendar

---

[4]BOP has established performance-based contracts with four private corrections companies. The private prisons in which BOP houses federal inmates operate in accordance with BOP policies.

[5]Rated capacity is the maximum population level at which an institution can make available basic necessities, essential services (e.g., medical care), and programs (e.g., drug treatment, basic education, and vocational education). According to BOP officials, by contract with BOP, privately run prisons cannot exceed 15 percent overcapacity. BOP also has agreements with state and local governments and contracts with privately operated facilities for the detention of federally adjudicated juveniles and for the secure detention of some short-term federal inmates.

[6]Unless noted otherwise, the term "crowding" in this report refers to BOP's definition.

[7]The Federal Managers' Financial Integrity Act, Pub. L. No. 97-255, 96 Stat. 814 (1982), assessment process evaluates the effectiveness of internal controls to support effective and efficient program operations, reliable financial reporting, compliance with applicable laws and regulations, and whether financial management systems conform to financial system requirements.

[8]Since 1998, the IG has prepared lists of top management challenges for the department. By statute, the Attorney General is required to include each year's list in the annual performance and accountability report.

years 1977 through 2008, with the first decline of 0.2 percent (2,857 prisoners) occurring in 2009. DOJ reported a second-year decline in 2010 of 0.8 percent (10,881 prisoners), with 25 states reporting decreases in their prison populations.[9] While not all states experienced reductions in their prison populations, in those states that did, changes in those states' policies and practices are potential contributing factors to this decline. According to a 2008 study by the Pew Center on the States, a state may reduce its prison population growth while protecting public safety by (1) diverting a greater number of low-risk offenders from prison, (2) reducing the time that low-risk offenders are in prison, or (3) a combination of these approaches.[10] In contrast to the prison populations of the states, the federal prison population has continued to grow. BOP is required by statute to provide for suitable housing and the safekeeping, care, and subsistence of all persons charged with or convicted of offenses against the United States.[11] Thus, while the size of a prison population is, in part, a function of crime rates, sentencing laws, and law enforcement policies, these factors are all beyond BOP's control. BOP's population is expected to continually increase, given current incarceration rates, and safety and security concerns will remain paramount.

We have previously reported on BOP's population projections, the security and safety of inmates and staff, and inmate programs.[12] For example, in November 2009, having assessed how BOP developed its population projections and compared its projections with its actual inmate population growth from fiscal years 1999 through August 20, 2009, we concluded that BOP's projections were accurate, on average, to within 1 percent of the actual inmate population growth during this time period.[13] In February 2012, we reported on BOP's use of its discretionary authority

---

[9]See Department of Justice, Bureau of Justice Statistics, *Prisoners in 2010* (Washington, D.C.: December 2011), and *Prisoners in 2009* (Washington, D.C.: December 2010).

[10]The Pew Center on the States, *One in 100: Behind Bars in America* 2008 (Washington, D.C.: February 2008). The Pew Center on the States provides nonpartisan reporting and research, advocacy, and technical assistance to help states deliver better results. Among the issues it addresses are heath, the economy, revenue and spending, and public safety.

[11]18 U.S.C. § 4042(a)(2).

[12]See Related GAO Products at the end of this report.

[13]GAO, *Bureau of Prisons: Methods for Cost Estimation Largely Reflect Best Practices but Quantifying Risks Would Enhance Decision Making*, GAO-10-94 (Washington, D.C.: Nov.10, 2009).

to reduce a prisoner's period of incarceration.[14] We recommended that BOP establish a plan, including time frames and milestones, for requiring contractors to submit separate prices of beds in residential reentry centers—also known as halfway houses—and home detention services. BOP concurred and has actions under way to address the recommendation.

You asked us to review the impact of crowding in BOP facilities and any related lessons that BOP can learn from selected states. Specifically, this report addresses the following questions:

1. What was the growth in BOP's population from fiscal years 2006 through 2011, and what are BOP's projections for inmate population and capacity?

2. What is known about the effects of a growing federal prison population on operations (i.e., inmates, staff, and infrastructure) within BOP facilities, and to what extent has BOP taken actions to mitigate these effects?

3. What actions have selected states taken to reduce their prison populations, and to what extent has BOP implemented similar initiatives?

To address the first question, we analyzed policies and procedures that may affect the increased federal prison population (e.g., BOP's inmate classification policy) and BOP's statutory authority affecting its capacity and conditions of confinement. We also analyzed BOP's inmate population data and crowding percentages by institutional security level from fiscal years 2006 through 2011 and BOP's 2020 long-range capacity plan, which was issued in January 2012. We assessed the reliability of BOP's inmate population and crowding data by reviewing relevant documentation, interviewing knowledgeable agency officials about how they maintain the integrity of their data, and updating previous assessments that we did for previously issued reports. We found BOP's inmate population and crowding data to be sufficiently reliable for the

---

[14]For GAO reports on federal prisons, see, for example: GAO, *Bureau of Prisons: Eligibility and Capacity Impact Use of Flexibilities to Reduce Inmates' Time in Prison*, GAO-12-320 (Washington, D.C. Feb. 7, 2012).

purposes of this report. We also interviewed BOP headquarters officials to discuss how BOP's population has grown.

To address the second question, we analyzed BOP's statutory authority, policies, and procedures pertinent to the effects of the growing population on operations in BOP facilities (i.e., effects on inmates, staff, and infrastructure) and BOP's ability to mitigate the effects of a growing population. We also analyzed BOP studies on the effects of population growth and prison crowding on BOP operations, as well as BOP data from fiscal years 2006 through 2011 on available bed space, inmate program participation and waiting lists, inmate-to-staff ratios, and available infrastructure costs. We also present systemwide BOP staffing ratios from fiscal years 1997 through 2011 because officials believed that presenting the ratios for a longer period better illustrates the effect of BOP's population growth relative to the number of staff.[15] We assessed the reliability of BOP's inmate, staff, and infrastructure data by interviewing knowledgeable agency officials to determine how BOP collects and maintains the integrity of these data. We found these data to be sufficiently reliable for the purposes of this report. We visited 5 of BOP's 117 prisons that are located in four of BOP's six regions, which we chose on the basis of varying security levels and to ensure geographic dispersion.[16] Because we did not randomly select the prisons we visited, our results are not generalizable to all BOP prisons; however, they provided important insights into BOP's operations. We interviewed BOP headquarters officials and all six regional directors. Further, we discussed the effects of BOP's population growth on correctional staff with officials from the Council of Prison Locals, the union that represents all nonmanagement staff working in BOP facilities.

To also address the second as well as the third question, we compared and contrasted BOP's actions to mitigate the effects of its increased population and attempt to reduce its prison population with similar actions taken by five selected states—Kansas, Mississippi, New York, Ohio, and Wisconsin—that had experienced prison population growth and had

---

[15]According to BOP officials, BOP also includes this information in its annual congressional budget request.

[16]We selected five federal prisons of different security levels, including one that was a complex and on whose grounds there was a low and a medium security facility. Thus, our five selected sites included six BOP facilities—one low, three medium, one high, and one administrative. We describe the distinctions among security levels later in this report.

taken actions to mitigate its effects or reduce their prison populations. To select the states, among other things, we reviewed the Bureau of Justice Statistics's (BJS) report on state prison inmate populations in 2010.[17] We also reviewed relevant reports on actions that states have taken to mitigate the effects of their prison population growth, published from 2006 through 2011 (e.g., those from the Pew Center on the States). Further, we assessed the extent to which actions in these selected states would be possible for BOP to undertake within its statutory authority. We also conducted site visits to three facilities in two of these five states. Dissimilarities between federal and state prison systems—legally, structurally, and in how crowding calculations are determined—limit the comparability between federal and state correctional systems, but we mitigated this limitation by the criteria we used to select the states in our sample (e.g., size of the prison population and diverse approaches to addressing increased prison populations). We are unable to generalize about the types of actions states have taken to mitigate the effects of state prison population growth or reduce their prison populations, but the information we obtained provides examples of state responses to prison population growth. Appendix I includes more details about our scope and methodology.

We conducted this performance audit from September 2011 to September 2012 in accordance with generally accepted government auditing standards. Those standards require that we plan and perform the audit to obtain sufficient, appropriate evidence to provide a reasonable basis for our findings and conclusions based on our audit objectives. We believe that the evidence obtained provides a reasonable basis for our findings and conclusions based on our audit objectives.

Background

There are specific state and federal laws that define, prohibit, and penalize criminal behavior. Various factors, such as the nature and type of the crime committed and the relevant law, may determine whether the state or federal justice system is responsible for the prosecution, sentencing, and incarceration of an individual accused and found guilty of a crime. State and federal laws also define the potential sentences for those crimes to be imposed by judges and methods for reducing the period of incarceration, such as parole, probation, or good conduct time

---

[17]See BJS, *Prisoners in 2010* (Washington, D.C.: Dec. 2011).

credit. These laws and policies affect the growth of their respective prison populations and the level of crowding in state and federal prison populations.

Federal Prison System

To carry out its responsibility for the custody and care of federal offenders, BOP currently houses inmates across six geographic regions in 117 federal institutions, 15 privately managed prisons, 185 residential reentry centers, and home detention.[18] BOP's central office consists of eight divisions that provide oversight of major BOP program areas and operations, such as correctional programs and health services, as well as the National Institute of Corrections (NIC).[19] BOP has six regional offices, each led by a regional director, covering the Mid-Atlantic, North Central, Northeast, South Central, Southeast, and Western regions of the United States.

BOP generally houses sentenced inmates in its long-term institutions. Male long-term institutions include four security level designations—minimum, low, medium, and high—and female institutions include three security designations—minimum, secure, and high.[20] The security level designation of a facility depends on the level of security and staff supervision that the institution is able to provide, such as the presence of security towers; perimeter barriers; the type of inmate housing, including dormitory, cubicle, or cell-type housing; and inmate-to-staff ratio. Additionally, BOP designates some of its institutions as administrative institutions, which specifically serve inmates awaiting trial, or those with intensive medical or mental health conditions, regardless of the level of supervision these inmates require.[21] From fiscal years 2006 through

---

[18]According to BOP officials, privately managed contract facilities are low security and primarily house non-U.S. citizens convicted of crimes while in this country legally or illegally. Home detention describes all circumstances under which an inmate is serving a portion of his or her sentence while residing in his or her home.

[19]NIC, a component of BOP, provides training, technical assistance, information services, and policy/program development assistance to federal, state, and local corrections agencies.

[20]In this report, data presented by institutional security level include information for male inmates by the four security levels and for females by the three security levels. Unless noted, these data do not include information on detention, medical, administrative, or Witness Security Program housing.

[21]The Administrative Maximum (ADX) facility in Florence, Colorado, houses offenders requiring the tightest controls.

2011, the distribution of facilities by security designation remained relatively constant. In fiscal year 2011, there were 7 stand-alone minimum security camps, 29 low security facilities, 46 medium security facilities, 16 high security facilities, and 19 administrative facilities.[22]

BOP establishes a rated capacity for each of the facilities that it owns and operates.[23] A facility's rated capacity reflects the number of prisoners that it was designed to house safely and securely and in which BOP can provide inmates adequate access to services, necessities for daily living, and programs designed to support their crime-free return to the community.[24] In determining a facility's rated capacity, BOP considers American Correctional Association (ACA) occupancy and space requirements.[25] Since 1990, ACA has required 35 square feet of unencumbered space per inmate to ensure that each inmate has sufficient movement or exercise space within the inmate's personal living space, whether in a cell, room, or open dormitory. In essence, rated capacity is the measure of inmate housing space and, therefore, does not include housing used for medical and special housing purposes (e.g., disciplinary segregation and administrative detention space). BOP also does not include in its rated capacity additional beds placed in areas such as a facility's halls, gyms, mezzanines, or television rooms to address crowding. BOP excludes this use of space from its rated capacity calculation because it considers these beds to be temporarily converted housing space that is to be restored to its original purpose when circumstances permit. Further, for such temporary space to become permanent space and thus included in a facility's rated capacity, the

---

[22]BOP has 7 stand-alone minimum security camps that are not colocated with higher security level facilities. BOP also has 73 minimum security satellite camps that are colocated with a secure institution or complex. Stand-alone camps usually have a rated capacity of 256 inmates, and colocated camps usually have a rated capacity of 128 inmates. Female secure facilities are included in the low security level facility figure.

[23]BOP does not include privately contracted beds as part of its systemwide rated capacity, because the capacity of each of these facilities is based on its contract.

[24]Basic necessities include safety, living space, and access to toilets, showers, and food. Essential services include medical care, visitation, and telephones to allow contact with family and other members of the community. Programs include drug treatment, work, education, vocational training, anger management, and parenting to prevent idleness and enable inmates to develop skills needed to return to the community following release.

[25]ACA's mission includes the development and promotion of effective standards for the care, custody, training, and treatment of offenders.

         GAO-12-743 Federal Prison Crowding

facility would require infrastructure changes, such as additional toilet or shower facilities, to meet ACA standards.

According to BOP, rated capacity is the basis for measuring prison crowding and is essential to both managing the inmate population and BOP's budget justifications for capital resources. BOP's formula for calculating rated capacity has changed over time. Until 1991, the rated capacity of a facility was equivalent to the total number of cells, because the rated capacity was based on one inmate being housed in each cell. As a result of the growth in BOP's population during the 1980s, BOP began to double-bunk (i.e., house two inmates in each cell) in many of its facilities, particularly those at the lower security levels. In 1991, BOP established a new rated capacity formula that allowed for stratified bunking across all security levels. BOP's current rated capacity guidelines account for

- 25 percent double bunking and 75 percent single bunking of cells within high security facilities,

- 50 percent double bunking and 50 percent single bunking of cells within medium security facilities, and

- 100 percent double bunking of cells in low and minimum security facilities.

By way of illustration, figure 1 shows crowding in a medium security facility and a high security facility, each with 20 cells. The rated capacity of the medium security facility, which includes 50 percent double bunking, is 30 beds. With a population of 45 inmates, 67 percent of the inmates are double bunked, 33 percent are triple bunked, and the facility's percentage crowding is 50 percent. The rated capacity of the high security facility, which includes 25 percent double bunking, is 25 beds. With a population of 39 inmates, 97 percent of the inmates are double bunked, 3 percent are single bunked, and the facility's percentage crowding is 56 percent.

Figure 1: Illustration of a 20-Cell Medium Security Facility with 45 Inmates and 50 Percent Crowding and a 20-Cell High Security Facility with 39 Inmates and 56 Percent Crowding

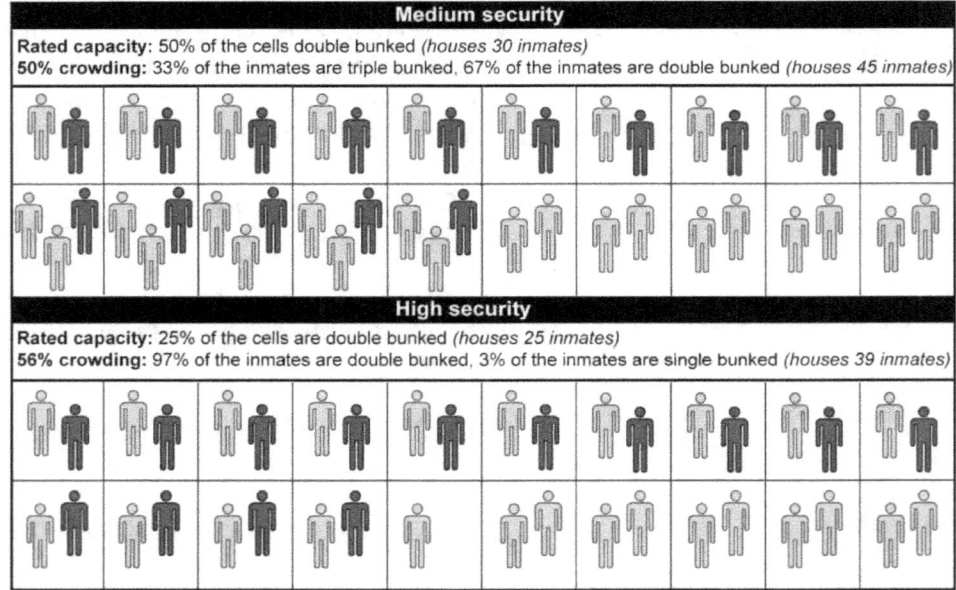

Legend:

Inmates per cell at rated capacity

Additional inmates per cell with crowding

Source: GAO analysis of BOP's fiscal year 2013 congressional budget submission.

BOP initially classifies an inmate to a particular institution based on

- the level of security and supervision the inmate requires;

- the level of security and staff supervision the institution is able to provide;

- the inmate's program needs, such as residential drug treatment or intensive medical care;[26]

- where the inmate resides when sentenced;

- the level of crowding in an institution; and

- any additional security measures to ensure the protection of victims, witnesses, and the public.

In most cases, BOP's Designation and Sentence Computation Center staff calculates a point score for the inmate and then matches the inmate with a commensurate security level institution.[27]

As of December 31, 2011, BOP had a total staff of about 38,000, including correctional officers[28] and administrative, program, and support personnel responsible for all of BOP's activities nationwide.[29] BOP's philosophy is that all employees are correctional workers first, whether or not they serve as correctional officers. Accordingly, BOP trains all employees in basic correctional duties to secure the facility in the event of a disturbance and to provide inmate supervision. BOP also requires them to participate in annual refresher training.[30] When circumstances warrant, a warden will require program and administrative staff members to serve in the capacity of a correctional officer—a practice that BOP calls augmentation. For example, under augmentation, a vocational education teacher or a psychologist may provide escort services for an inmate

---

[26]For prior work related to BOP's implementation of Second Chance Act provisions, which affect programming needs related to preparing inmates for eventual reentry into society, see GAO, *Federal Bureau of Prisons: BOP Has Mechanisms in Place to Address Most Second Chance Act Requirements and Is Working to Implement an Initiative Designed to Reduce Recidivism*, GAO-10-854R (Washington, D.C.: July 14, 2010).

[27]See GAO-12-320.

[28]Correctional officers enforce the regulations governing the operation of a correctional institution, serving as both supervisors and counselors of inmates.

[29]These staff included all staff on-board funded under BOP's appropriation for Salaries and Expenses (i.e., headquarters, regional, institutional, and Public Health Service staff), as well as Buildings and Facilities, Commissary, and Federal Prison Industries staff.

[30]See GAO, *Bureau of Prisons: Evaluating the Impact of Protective Equipment Could Help Enhance Officer Safety*, GAO-11-410 (Washington, D.C.: Apr. 8, 2011).

leaving the facility for specialized medical care or provide ancillary supervision in a recreational yard.

State Prison Systems

Selected state departments of corrections included in our review share similarities and exhibit differences with BOP. For example, both state departments of corrections and BOP are required to house, clothe, and feed inmates in a safe and secure setting, but selected states determine rated capacity and measure crowding differently. Several of the selected state departments of corrections' methods are different from BOP's methods. For example, New York calculates rated capacity using standards set forth by the New York State Commission of Correction and by subtracting temporary beds from the number of general population beds. In contrast, Wisconsin does not calculate rated capacity but instead uses design capacity and operational capacity.[31] Furthermore, differences in state and federal authorities affect the types of actions that are taken to mitigate the effects of crowding. For example, state departments of corrections may have been granted certain state statutory authorities that are not currently available at the federal level (i.e., states may transfer inmates to county and local jails, but BOP does not have this option).

BOP's Population Grew More than Systemwide Capacity, and BOP Projects Continued Population Growth through 2020

From fiscal years 2006 through 2011, the inmate population in BOP-run facilities grew 9.5 percent, while capacity grew less than 7 percent. As a result, BOP's overall crowding increased during this period from 36 percent to 39 percent. BOP projects an additional 15 percent increase in its inmate population by 2020.

---

[31]Design capacity is the number of inmates that planners intended for a facility. Operational capacity is the number of inmates that can be accommodated based on a facility's staff, existing programs, and services.

BOP's Population Grew Steadily because of a Variety of Factors

The inmate population housed in BOP-run facilities steadily increased from 162,514 to 177,934 inmates—or 9.5 percent—from fiscal years 2006 through 2011.[32] A variety of factors contribute to the size of BOP's population. These include national crime levels, law enforcement policies, and federal sentencing laws, all of which are beyond BOP's control. During the 6-year period, growth occurred in BOP's male, female, and both its U.S. citizen and non-U.S. citizen populations. Specifically,

- The number of male inmates housed in BOP institutions increased about 10 percent (151,003 to 165,595).

- The number of female inmates housed in BOP institutions increased about 7 percent (11,511 to 12,339).

- The relative proportion of non-U.S. citizen to U.S. citizen inmates housed in BOP facilities remained constant (about 26 percent), although the approximately 16 percent (46,369 to 53,733) growth in the noncitizen inmate population surpassed the approximate 13 percent growth in the U.S. citizen inmate population (135,074 to 152,581).[33]

  - Non-U.S. citizen inmates are housed in BOP-run low, medium, and high security level facilities, as well as in private contract facilities.[34]

  - The largest number of these inmates are housed in low security facilities.

---

[32]These data include only those U.S. inmates housed in BOP-run facilities, not privately contracted facilities.

[33]These data include only those U.S. citizen or non-U.S. citizen inmates housed in BOP-run facilities. The total number of non-U.S. citizen inmates, including those housed in BOP-run and private contract facilities, increased about 13 percent (50,275 to 56,933) from fiscal years 2006 through 2011, and constituted about 26 percent of the total BOP population during this time period.

[34]BOP does not send non-U.S. citizen inmates to minimum security facilities because of their risk of flight.

- Drug, weapons/explosives, and immigration offenses constituted the largest number of offenses for which all BOP inmates were incarcerated in each year from fiscal years 2006 through 2011.[35] Specifically, in fiscal year 2011,

  - 48 percent of the inmates BOP housed were serving sentences for drugs,

  - 16 percent for weapons/explosives, and

  - 12 percent for immigration.

Appendix II provides additional information on the growth of the federal inmate population from fiscal years 2006 through 2011 and the other offense categories for which BOP inmates have been sentenced.

Rated Capacity Grew Less than 7 Percent, Contributing to Crowding

BOP's 9.5 percent population growth from fiscal years 2006 through 2011 among inmates housed in BOP facilities exceeded the increase in its rated capacity, which grew less than 7 percent (from 119,510 beds to 127,795). BOP's rated capacity during this 6-year period grew because it opened five new facilities and closed four stand-alone minimum security camps, which BOP officials told us were less efficient to operate. As shown in figure 2, however, because the inmate population in BOP-run facilities grew at a faster rate than the growth in rated capacity, crowding in BOP-run institutions increased from 36 to 39 percent systemwide.

---

[35]BOP officials explained that for reporting purposes, they categorize inmates according to the offense for which an inmate is serving the longest sentence (dominant sentence offense). For example, an inmate may be serving sentences for both drug and immigration offenses, but BOP will categorize the inmate by the offense having the longer sentence (e.g., the drug offense).

Figure 2: BOP Systemwide Population, Rated Capacity, and Percentage Crowding from Fiscal Years 2006 through 2011

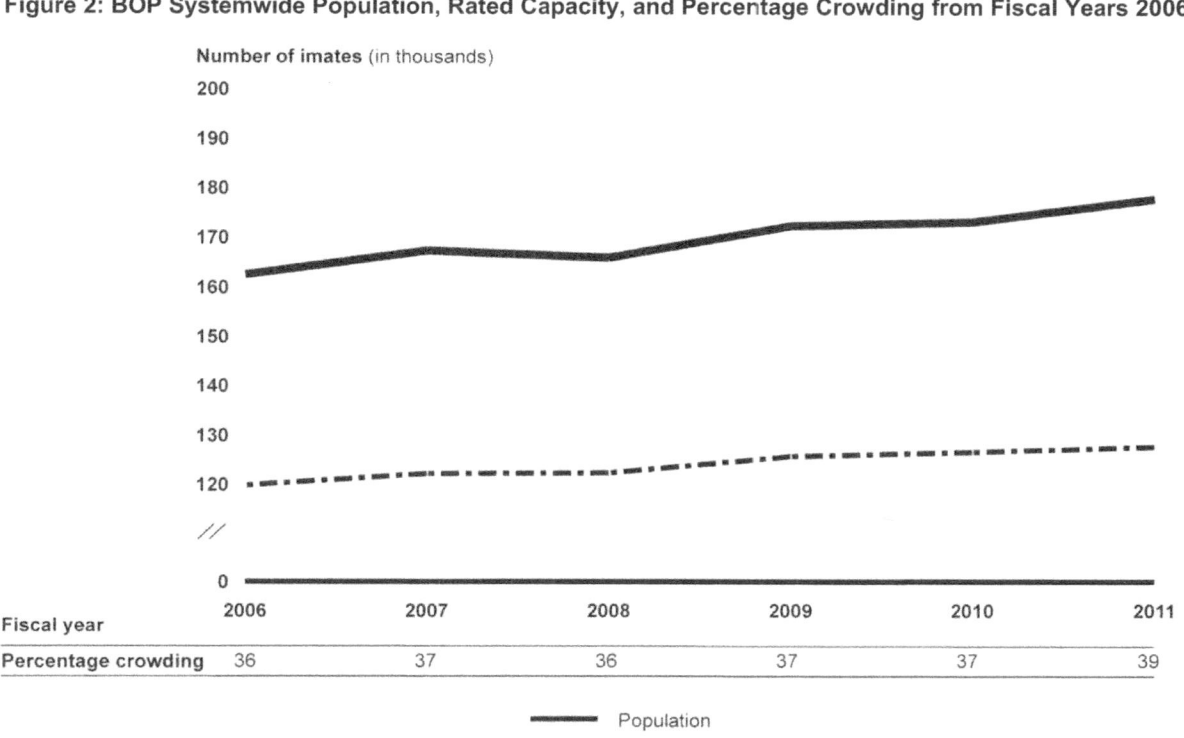

Fiscal year	2006	2007	2008	2009	2010	2011
Percentage crowding	36	37	36	37	37	39

——— Population

— ·— · Rated capacity

Source: GAO analysis of BOP data.

From fiscal years 2006 through 2011, the percentage crowding in male medium security facilities increased from 37 percent to 51 percent and from 53 percent to 55 percent in high security level facilities. Table 5 in appendix II illustrates the range of crowding across BOP institutions of different security levels as of December 2011, and the double, triple, and quadruple bunking that has resulted. For example, the population in BOP's high security population was about 21,000 in December 2011—or about 7,000 more than its rated capacity—resulting in 97 percent double bunking and a 55 percentage crowding.

According to BOP, BOP's ability to increase rated capacity is directly affected by funding appropriated for new prison construction and to support contracts with private prison providers for additional inmate bed space. In fiscal year 2005, the Office of Management and Budget (OMB) placed a moratorium on all new BOP prison construction. To address BOP's bed space needs, OMB focused on contracting with private prisons. BOP officials stated that, because of this moratorium, the yearly presidential budget submissions for BOP's Buildings and Facilities account for each of fiscal years 2006 through 2011 did not include requests to begin construction on any new facilities. Instead, the Buildings and Facilities requests included what BOP considers to be baseline funding[36] for ongoing expenses, which were generally about $25 million during each of the 6 fiscal years in this period.[37] Congress, however, provided about $1.1 billion specifically to aid in the site selection, design, and construction of new BOP facilities—in addition to funding the baseline that BOP requested. According to BOP officials, the time from receiving the funding appropriation to building and opening—or activating—a facility is generally 3 to 5 years.

In addition, according to BOP officials, funding was requested and provided to contract for private bed space during this period—with the exception of fiscal years 2008 and 2011. BOP officials explained that only low security inmates can be housed in privately managed facilities; thus, in years when BOP has received related funds, they have been able to move these lower security inmates to the contracted facilities. However, since they have not consistently received this money, BOP officials told us they designated some low security inmates to medium security facilities. As a result, BOP is currently housing 4,500 low security inmates in medium security facilities, contributing to crowding at that security level.

BOP officials said that housing low security inmates in medium security institutions is contributing to crowding in medium security institutions, but BOP's low security facilities are "just plain full."

According to BOP data, 81 percent of male inmates housed in low security facilities were triple bunked at the end of 2011. Officials noted that if they were able to add more contract beds they could reduce crowding in medium and low security facilities by moving (1) non-U.S.

[36]BOP's Building and Facilities budgetary account includes two "decision units"—one for "new construction" and one for "maintenance and repair." Within the "new construction" decision unit, baseline funding includes about $10 million annually to support the lease payments on BOP's federal inmate transfer center, as well as other costs associated with considering potential construction sites, studying environmental impact, and any facility expansion and conversion projects. These baseline funds also cover the salaries and administrative costs of architects, project managers, and procurement and other staff necessary to carry out the efforts.

[37]During this period, the fiscal year 2008 budget submission was the outlier, when the request included $115 million to support construction that had already begun at the Mendota facility. Congress ultimately appropriated these funds, but did so as part of the fiscal year 2007 budget. Because of protracted budget negotiations in fiscal year 2007, the budget that year passed after the fiscal year 2008 budget had been submitted.

citizen inmates from low security facilities to contract facilities and (2) low security inmates from medium security facilities to low security facilities. (See table 6 in app. II for additional data on BOP's population growth, rated capacity, and percentage crowding data for fiscal years 2006 through 2011.)

BOP Projects Continued Population Growth

BOP's 2020 long-range capacity plan assumes continued growth in the federal prison population from fiscal years 2011 through 2020, with about 15 percent growth in the number of inmates BOP will house.[38] To address some of this growth, BOP expects to activate five newly constructed prisons by 2014, adding about 6,720 beds.[39] In addition, BOP is budgeting for additional contracted bed space—1,000 beds in 2013 and 1,500 the next year, but the addition of these contracted beds is subject to future appropriations. Despite its plans to add capacity through 2014, given the expected inmate population growth, BOP projects crowding will increase from the current rate of 39 percent to 44 percent by 2015.

Beyond 2015, BOP projects it will be able to bring crowding in BOP facilities down to 35 percent by 2020. BOP's projections assume that BOP will receive additional funding for constructing new facilities. Specifically, BOP assumes an overall increase of over 17,500 beds from fiscal years 2016 through 2020, generally as a result of opening new high and medium security facilities, none of which is under construction. BOP has not requested funding for this additional bed space, and as a result, its plans are contingent on the budget development and appropriations processes and are subject to change. Appendix II provides additional information on BOP's population growth from fiscal years 2006 through 2011 and projections from fiscal years 2012 through 2020.

---

[38]These projections are from BOP's 2020 capacity plan dated January 10, 2012. In November 2009, we concluded that BOP's projections at the time were accurate, on average, to within 1 percent of the actual inmate population growth from fiscal year 1999 through August 20, 2009. See GAO-10-94.

[39]According to BOP, these facilities include two medium security/camp facilities in Mendota, California (1,152 beds) and Berlin, New Hampshire (1,280 beds), that will open from 2012 through 2013; one female secure/low security camp facility in Aliceville, Alabama (1,792 beds), opening from 2012 through 2014; and one medium security/camp facility in Hazelton, West Virginia (1,280 beds); and one high security facility in Yazoo City, Mississippi (1,216 beds), scheduled to open from 2013 through 2014.

BOP's Population Growth Has Negatively Affected Inmates, Staff, and Infrastructure, but BOP Has Acted to Help Mitigate These Effects

According to BOP and our observations, the growth of the federal inmate population and related crowding have negatively affected inmates housed in BOP institutions, institutional staff, and the infrastructure of BOP facilities, and have contributed to inmate misconduct, which affects staff and inmate security and safety. Nevertheless, BOP officials said that it is difficult to demonstrate or isolate the effects of crowding, per se, as distinguished from population growth or other factors such as staffing levels.

Impacts of Population Growth

Inmates

The growth in the inmate population affects inmates' daily living conditions, program participation, meaningful work opportunities, and visitation. Appendix III describes each in greater detail, and we present some highlights here.

Daily Living

To increase available bed space, BOP reports double bunking in excess of the percentages included in a facility's rated capacity; triple and quadruple bunking; or converting common space, such as a television room, temporarily to housing space. As a result of BOP actions to increase available bed space in its institutions to accommodate the growing federal inmate population, more inmates are sharing cells and other living units, which brings together for longer periods of time inmates with a higher risk of violence and more potential victims.[40] Table 8 in appendix III illustrates the use of temporary beds by institutional security level, and shows, for example, that temporary beds, not including those used for disciplinary purposes, composed about 29 percent of the bed space in male high security facilities in fiscal year 2011. According to BOP headquarters officials, wardens have discretion to provide temporary beds by adding a third bunk within cells, converting a television room to bed space, or using both approaches. The facility's infrastructure also

---

[40]BOP. *The Effects of Changing Crowding and Staffing Levels in Federal Prisons on Inmate Violence Rates—Executive Summary* (Washington, D.C.: October 2005).

affects the approach the warden may implement. For example, the smaller cells in older BOP facilities make it more difficult to add a third bed, while the larger cells in newer facilities can be triple-bunked. The officials noted, however, that triple-bunking all cells in a unit presents a challenge to staff who have to manage the large number of inmates. Additionally, a regional director may have a preferred approach to providing temporary beds within his or her region. Figure 3 illustrates some of the options used.

Figure 3: Examples of BOP's Use of Temporary Bed Space

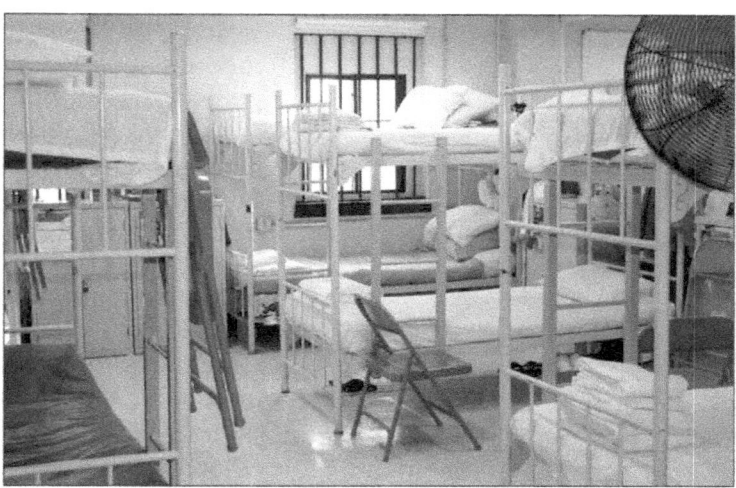

Source: BOP.

All of the BOP facilities we visited reported using temporary beds from fiscal years 2006 through 2011 and continue to do so. At the time of our site visits in 2011 and 2012, these facilities continued to use temporary space. For example, we observed triple-bunked cells in a low security facility and a converted television room that housed 10 inmates in a medium security facility. In addition to experiencing crowding in a facility's housing and common areas, inmates may experience crowded bathroom facilities, reductions in shower times, shortened meal times coupled with longer waits for food service, and more limited recreational activities because of the increased inmate population.

Program Participation

According to BOP officials, the growth in the inmate population affects the availability of program opportunities, resulting in waiting lists and inmate idleness. BOP provides programs including education, vocational training, drug treatment, and faith-based reentry programs that help to rehabilitate inmates and support correctional management.[41] BOP officials said that two long-term benefits of inmate programming are (1) public safety, attributable to enhanced inmate skill sets that can reduce future crime and inmate rearrest rates, and (2) institutional safety and security because of reduced inmate idleness.

According to BOP officials, facility staff provide a range of education programs, including mandatory General Educational Development (GED) courses; 8- to 10-week nonmandatory courses on topics such as parenting, word processing, and conversational Spanish; occupational training; and computer-based self-paced courses such as English. BOP reported that overall inmate participation in one or more programs was 36 percent in September 2011 (see table 10 in app. III).[42] BOP also offers residential drug abuse treatment in more than half of its facilities and nonresidential drug abuse and drug education programs in all of its facilities. The percentage of participation, number of inmates on waiting lists, and length of the average waiting time varied by program. As tables 11 through 13 in appendix III illustrate, all of the drug treatment and drug education programs had waiting lists from fiscal years 2006 through 2011. For example, as of the end of fiscal year 2011, about 2,400 inmates in male medium security institutions participated in residential drug treatment, almost 3,000 more inmates were on the waiting list to participate, and the average wait for enrollment exceeded 3 months. According to BOP officials, if BOP cannot meet the substance abuse treatment or education needs of inmates because it does not have the staff needed to meet program demand, some inmates will not receive programming benefits. As we reported in February 2012, long waiting lists for BOP's Residential Drug Abuse Program (RDAP), which provides sentence reductions for eligible inmates who successfully complete the program,[43] constrained BOP's ability to admit participants early enough to

---

[41]See GAO-01-483.

[42]BOP's Monthly Participation Reports provide a snapshot of program participation levels of inmates within BOP facilities. Figures for overall inmate participation do not duplicate. That is, if an inmate is enrolled in more than one program area (for example GED and parenting), the inmate's participation is counted only once.

[43]28 C.F.R. § 550.53(b) outlines the RDAP eligibility criteria. 28 C.F.R. § 550.55 outlines eligibility for early release.

earn their maximum allowable reductions in times served.[44] From fiscal years 2009 through 2011, BOP expanded RDAP capacity by 400 slots. Though wait times for enrollment have declined, the program continues to experience long waiting lists.

Meaningful Work Opportunities

According to BOP headquarters officials, the growth in the federal inmate population has also affected inmate work opportunities, as it is difficult to find meaningful work for all inmates, even though generally all inmates are required to have a job.[45] BOP inmates participate in a variety of jobs. For example, at facilities we visited, we observed inmate workers preparing meals under the supervision of staff, sweeping the floors, and working in a factory that produced and printed a variety of government publications. BOP officials explained, however, that with the growth of the prison population, fewer opportunities exist to engage in meaningful work. This makes it difficult for staff to keep inmates busy, resulting in inmate idleness, which can lead to additional tension and fighting between inmates. For example, officials at one facility told us that more inmates than needed may be assigned to a task and paid the same wage, but consequently, not everyone is engaged and equally busy.

Visitation

According to BOP headquarters officials, the quality of the interaction between an inmate and family can positively affect an inmate's behavior in prison and aids an inmate's success when returning to the community; however, crowded visiting rooms make it more difficult for inmates to visit with their families. Each BOP facility has visiting space to accommodate the number of inmates that the facility was designed to house and a visitor capacity to enable staff to manage the visitation process. The infrastructure of the facility may not support the increase in visitors as a result of the growth in the prison population. For example, at one older facility we visited, officials said that the number of visitors was so great and the visiting room was so small that visitors had to wait hours to get into the visiting room.

---

[44]For more on RDAP, see GAO-12-320.

[45]The Crime Control Act of 1990, Pub. L. No. 101-647, § 2905, 104 Stat. 4789, 4914 (codified at 18 U.S.C. § 4121 note) established a mandatory work requirement for all federal prisoners. A prisoner may be excused from this requirement only as necessitated by security considerations; disciplinary action; medical certification of disability; or a need to work less than a full schedule in order to participate in literacy training, drug rehabilitation, or similar programs in addition to the work program.

Staff

BOP headquarters officials said that with the primary exception of hiring staff when a new facility opens, the number of staff positions generally has not increased as BOP's population has grown, affecting staff stress and overtime hours worked. BOP officials explained that BOP is required to feed, clothe, and provide medical care for inmates. After these costs are met, BOP funds staffing levels to the extent possible. As a result, BOP headquarters officials confirmed that overall staffing in BOP facilities systemwide is on average less than 90 percent of authorized levels, varying by the facility's location. For example, a warden may staff correctional programs at the 97 percent level and the business office at the 60 percent level. In addition to funding, BOP officials identified recruitment challenges that affected staffing levels. For example, one regional director said that finding qualified staff to hire was an ongoing issue in his region because generally applicants did not meet BOP's requirements. At two facilities we visited, officials noted that hiring professional staff (e.g., psychologists or medical staff) was difficult because BOP salaries were less than those paid in the community for the same position.

The increased inmate-to-staff ratio can increase staff overtime and stress and reduce inmate and staff communication. This can affect the safety and security of the institution as a whole.

From fiscal years 1997 through 2011, BOP reported that the systemwide ratio of inmates to all BOP staff (i.e., at BOP headquarters, regional offices, institutions, and training centers) increased from 3.57:1 to 4.94:1.[46] This is not the only staffing ratio BOP calculates however. In addition, BOP calculates a ratio of inmates and institutional staff within its facilities.[47] From fiscal years 2006 through 2011, the inmate to total institutional staff ratio for all facilities systemwide and for all male facilities was generally 5.2:1. In fiscal year 2011, this ratio was lower in high security facilities (4.1:1) and higher in low and minimum security facilities

[46]BOP calculates the ratio for inmates and all BOP staff at the systemwide level; not by security level. The inmate population is the actual population at each facility on the last day of the fiscal year. The staffing level is the total number of staff on board as of the last pay period of the fiscal year and includes all staff funded by BOP's Salaries and Expenses appropriations and Public Health Service staff at BOP headquarters, regional offices, institutions, and, training centers.

[47]In fiscal year 2005, BOP began calculating overall institutional staffing ratios on the basis of (1) all staff under BOP's Salaries and Expenses appropriations, including correctional officers, noncustody staff (e.g., teachers, psychologists, and administrative staff); and Public Health Service staff on board as of the last pay period of the fiscal year; and (2) the average inmate daily population at each BOP facility. These ratios exclude BOP Buildings and Facilities, Federal Prison Industries, Commissary, regional office, training center, and central office staff, as well as staff at facilities that were being activated.

(6.1:1 and 8.0:1, respectively). Further, BOP calculates a ratio of inmates to correctional officers. According to BOP, this ratio is 10:1 systemwide, but it varies depending on security level and mission of the facility. For example, in one Special Management Unit we visited, officials told us that there were about 6 inmates to each correctional officer.[48] This contrasted to a medium security facility where officials told us the ratio of inmates to correctional officers was 14:1.

According to an August 2010 DOJ study of BOP's staffing,[49] nearly all BOP facilities had fewer correctional staff on board than needed, with a BOP-wide staffing shortage in excess of 3,200.[50] Moreover, even if BOP filled all authorized positions, the study reported that the shortage would exceed 1,800. The study team observed that the institutional staff was very lean, highly functional, and adept at managing large numbers of inmates at a time, but there was also anecdotal evidence that understaffing was stressing the workforce. Thus, the study concluded that the systemwide inmate-to-staff ratio in BOP institutions—5.3:1 in 2009 when the study was prepared—must, at a minimum, be maintained.

Nevertheless, the study stated that BOP's use of a systemwide ratio had not been sufficiently effective in justifying additional annual budget requests, because the ratio did not convey operational realities at the institutional level. Specifically, the study found that there were variances in the number of daily correctional officer shifts based on the time of day and the day of the week that the overall ratio was not incorporating. Our observations illustrated this point. At one medium security facility we visited, officials reported a population of about 1,300 inmates, 56 percent crowding, an inmate to total staff ratio of 6.0:1. Facility officials explained,

---

[48]A Special Management Unit operates as a more controlled and restrictive environment for inmates whose interaction requires greater management to ensure the safety, security, or orderly operation of BOP facilities, or protection of the public.

[49]Justice Management Division, DOJ, *BOP Staffing Study* (Washington, D.C.: August 2010).

[50]According to the study. BOP uses a staffing roster to determine the number of correctional officers needed to fill custody posts at its facilities. The roster process identifies a clear need of correctional services personnel that is typically higher than the numbers of both funded and authorized positions. The study states that there appears to be a disconnect between (1) establishing authorized and funded staff positions and (2) determining the number of correctional officers needed to ensure institutional safety and security through BOP's staffing roster process.

however, that about 17 correctional officers were on duty during nights and evenings to supervise the general population. Thus, in contrast to the reported ratio, the actual inmate-to-staff ratio during these occasions was about 76:1. The DOJ study goes on to state that an inmate-to-staff ratio can provide a valuable perspective when it is used to show how staffing varies during specific shifts at specific institutions. When ratios are used in this context, decision makers can more effectively determine the appropriate number of institution staff needed to safely manage an institution. Accordingly, for BOP to justify its staffing levels plus additional resources for increased staff—as the inmate population grows—the study recommended, among other things, that BOP set a minimum inmate-to-staff ratio that is required to run a safe, secure, and efficient prison system given operational realties. Partly in response to the DOJ report, BOP officials said that they had developed minimum staffing guidelines, and as of June 2012, BOP was in the process of applying these guidelines at each facility. Tables 14-16 in appendix III illustrate the various inmate-to-staff ratios and trends over time.

BOP headquarters officials and the union representatives said that correctional staff worked more overtime hours to meet additional staff needs as a result of the larger inmate population.[51] Alternatively, in lieu of paying overtime, facility management may divert other professional or administration staff, as trained correctional officers, from their primary duties to supervise other aspects of inmate care and confinement, such as meal times or medical trips. According to BOP headquarters officials, this practice, known as augmentation, affects programming. For example, if a teacher has to fill a correctional post, then the class does not occur or another teacher may be required to supervise the course. Headquarters, regional, and facility officials said that they generally used augmentation during annual correctional officers' refresher training. For example, during our site visit to a Special Management Unit, we observed an administrative staff member serving as a correctional officer in the unit, replacing a correctional officer who was attending BOP-required annual

---

[51]For fiscal years 2009, 2010, and 2011, BOP reported a total of 1,480,713; 1,416,269.50; and 1,381,129.50 overtime hours charged by correctional officers in all facilities, respectively. BOP also maintains data on overtime costs for all BOP staff. Institutional overtime costs for all BOP regions totaled $102,877,891; $102,352,434; and $89,035,146 for each respective year. BOP officials said that the decline in fiscal year 2011 was due, in part, to reduced appropriations that year.

GAO-12-743 Federal Prison Crowding

staff refresher training.[52] BOP facilities and regional offices have tracked the use of augmentation, but headquarters did not review or analyze this information centrally until February 2012, at the direction of the new BOP Director. Therefore, during the course of our audit work, BOP could not provide any trend analysis on the use of augmentation systemwide.

Infrastructure

The increased population taxes the infrastructure that was designed for a smaller inmate population, affecting use of toilets, showers, water, and electricity, and wear and tear on food service equipment (e.g., freezer units). According to BOP headquarters and regional officials, crowding affects the general usage and upkeep of the facility, which affects the facility itself, the environment, and the local community.

BOP has also experienced increased maintenance and repair costs, with 51 facilities over 30 years old and newer facilities also in need of maintenance and repair.[53] BOP reported systemwide maintenance and repair costs of about $228 million in fiscal year 2006 and $262 million in fiscal year 2011—approximately a 15 percent increase. BOP headquarters officials stated that they are most concerned with "life safety issues," such as ensuring that sprinkler systems work properly in the event of fire in the facility. These officials said that requests for repairs are often put off when BOP does not receive funding. (See app. III for additional information on the effects of BOP's population growth on infrastructure.)

Security and Safety

BOP officials said the increasing inmate population and staffing ratios negatively affect inmate conduct and the imposition of discipline, thereby affecting security and safety. A 2005 BOP report on the effects of crowding and staffing levels in federal prisons on inmate violence rates concluded that population pressures on both staffing levels and inmate living space have an upward impact on serious prison violence. Nevertheless, the study also found that systemwide violence rates remained stable, although measures of both percent rated capacity and

---

[52]BOP established a Special Management Unit at Lewisburg Penitentiary in fiscal year 2008, and subsequently converted the entire facility to a Special Management Unit, with the exception of a unit housing general population high security inmates.

[53]In our previous work (GAO-10-94), we reported that BOP's methods for estimating costs in its annual budget requests largely reflect the four best practices outlined in GAO, *Cost Estimating and Assessment Guide: Best Practices for Developing and Managing Capital Program Costs,* GAO-09-3SP (Washington, D.C.: March 2009).

inmate to correctional officers ratios rose in federal prisons during the latter part of the study.[54] The study posits that this stability may stem from prison managers employing some operational practices, such as augmentation, that in the short term countered the negative effect of increased crowding. BOP officials told us that a follow-up to the 2005 study is not necessary because they did not believe that the findings would change.

BOP generally reported increases in the number of guilty findings for inmate misconduct from fiscal years 2006 through 2009, but the number of findings for misconduct of the greatest severity (e.g., killing, serious assault, and possession of weapons) began to decline in fiscal year 2010. Additionally, from fiscal years 2006 through 2011, BOP systemwide imposed almost 4,000 lockdowns—a temporary situation in which all inmates are confined to their living quarters/cells until staff are able to assess the situation following a critical incident (e.g., a disturbance, assaults on staff by several inmates, or a food or work strike) and can safely return the institution to normal operations. Similar to the inmate misconduct data, the number of lockdowns increased from fiscal years 2006 through 2009, and then began to decline. Appendix III provides information on BOP's disciplinary system and data on inmate misconduct and lockdowns.

BOP places inmates in **Special Housing Units** for disciplinary or administrative reasons when their presence in the general inmate population would otherwise threaten the safety, security, or orderly operation of the facility or potentially cause harm to the public. BOP places inmates in **Special Management Units** when inmates need an even more restrictive and controlled environment—for even longer terms—than can be offered in a Special Housing Unit or among the general inmate population.

BOP officials at all levels told us that they believe the establishment of Special Management Units beginning in fiscal year 2008 had contributed to the decrease in misconduct in the general population and the decline in the use of lockdowns, but that these facilities are too new to evaluate.[55] Nevertheless, BOP officials stated that its Special Management Units are now crowded and experiencing waiting lists.[56] Specifically, BOP reported that from March 1, 2012, through April 20, 2012, 231 inmates were approved for Special Management Unit placement and were awaiting a

---

[54]The study used calendar quarter data for 73 federal low, medium, and high security all male prisons from July 1996 through December 2004, a period of increased prison crowding and increased inmate to correctional officer ratios.

[55] We have ongoing work that focuses on BOP's Special Management Units and Special Housing Units. We expect to publish our results in early 2013. As part of our review, we are analyzing their effects on inmate misconduct.

[56]As of January 31, 2012, BOP reported housing 1,664 male inmates in its Special Management Units.

bed. The average wait time for placement in a Special Management Unit bed was 110 days.

Officials said that waiting lists for transfers to a Special Management Unit contribute to crowding in the facility Special Housing Unit. According to BOP officials, without space for disciplinary segregation, they are limited in how they can address inmate misconduct. Officials further stated that when a facility has no Special Housing Unit space available, the regional office may move the inmate to a Special Housing Unit in another facility of a different security level—a practice referred to as trans-segregation. Alternatively, headquarters officials said that disciplinary hearing officers may dispense shorter time in segregation or use other sanctions or a combination of nonsegregation sanctions. As a result, the officials said that the imposed sanctions may not be as much of a deterrent with the inmates, which affects the security and safety of inmates and staff.

BOP officials said they have both experienced and effective staff, but that they are reaching the highest crowding rates ever and have increasingly unfunded repair requests. They said that BOP cannot keep operating as it is without new capacity.

Additionally, BOP headquarters officials and union representatives we spoke with expressed concerns about future effects of increased inmate population growth. First, officials raised concern about the possibility of a serious incident occurring, especially at a high security or medium level facility. A serious incident could occur in a high security facility because these facilities are extremely crowded and house the most serious inmates (i.e., those who have committed the most serious crimes in society or in prison). A union representative also said that medium security facilities were at risk of an incident because these facilities lack the better lockdown procedures found in high security facilities. Nevertheless, BOP officials did not discount an incident happening at a low security facility because of the high gang presence in these facilities. They said that although the criminal histories of low security inmates suggest that they are not a "high risk" for violence, these inmates may still be a high risk for problems because of frustrations resulting from crowded conditions. Second, BOP officials were also concerned that the federal courts might require BOP to address conditions related to crowding or that ACA might revoke the accreditation of BOP institutions.[57]

BOP Has Worked to Increase Inmate and Staff Safety and Security and Has Reported Utilizing Resources More Efficiently

BOP has taken actions to manage a growing population within its facilities—and its approaches were similar to those in selected states we reviewed. These have generally been aimed at

- increasing inmate and staff safety and security and

- utilizing resources efficiently.

Efforts to Increase Inmate and Staff Safety and Security

Controlled inmate movement. BOP has implemented controlled movement for inmates, which is a practice that officials from one of the five states we reviewed also reported using, specifically to deal with crowded conditions. For example, because of crowded conditions, one way that BOP restricts inmates' movement in high and medium security facilities is by instituting earlier in-cell hours at night for inmates.[58] Further, BOP has a system of inmate movement in place to reduce potential tension and fighting and allow staff to better supervise inmates (i.e., staggering activities or meal times so that one cell block or unit of inmates proceeds at a time). Like officials at BOP, officials from Mississippi's Department of Corrections stagger recreational activities to curtail inmate fighting so that only one cell block or unit is released to the yard at a time.

Disciplinary housing. As previously discussed, because escalating tensions in crowded facilities can cause increased security concerns, BOP utilizes Special Housing Units to segregate inmates involved in

---

[57]In May 2011, the United States Supreme Court held in the case of *Brown, Governor of California, v. Plata*, 131 S.Ct. 1910, that a court-mandated prison inmate population limit was necessary to remedy the violation of a federal right, specifically the severe and unlawful mistreatment of prisoners through grossly inadequate provision of medical and mental health care. The Court recognized that for years the medical and mental health care provided by California's prisons had fallen short of minimum constitutional requirements and had failed to meet prisoners' basic health needs with needless suffering and death being the well-documented result. The Court stated that overcrowding had overtaken the limited resources of prison staff, imposed demands well beyond the capacity of medical and mental health facilities, and created unsanitary and unsafe conditions that made progress in the provision of care difficult or impossible to achieve.

[58]Controlled movement in high security facilities is often called restricted movement.

disciplinary infractions.[59] Officials in Kansas and New York also reported using disciplinary housing. BOP officials stated that the use of Special Housing Units has resulted in a decrease in inmate misconduct because those inciting tension within the general population have been removed.[60] According to a 2006 New York State Department of Correctional Services' report on prison safety, the department believed that the certainty of facing Special Housing Unit confinement for misbehavior contributed generally to improved inmate conduct, as reflected in inmates spending less time in these units without reductions in time to make room for other inmates.[61]

Preferential housing. To increase the safety and security of inmates and staff, BOP has encouraged positive behavior from inmates by rewarding them with preferential housing, and this was a practice we observed directly in a New York State Department of Corrections and Community Supervision facility. BOP officials described preferential housing as cells or dormitory rooms with fewer inmates than the facility's general population housing and located close to the phones or showers. BOP union officials stated that, at some facilities, preferential housing is given to inmates directly in response to their good behavior, and officials explained that inmates highly coveted these rewards and modified their behavior accordingly. For example, in one facility we visited, inmates in the cleanest unit were rewarded by getting to eat meals before inmates in other units. At one state facility we visited in New York, officials rewarded well-behaved inmates by allowing them to live in the "honor block"—a preferential housing unit that allows inmates more freedom of movement and additional personal decision making (e.g., inmates are allowed to decide when they wish to shower and do their laundry).

Expanded program options and incentives. To accommodate growing inmate populations, reduce inmate idleness, and help inmates prepare for life outside of prison—all of which relate to institutional safety—BOP

---

[59]As of January 31, 2012, BOP reported housing 11,624 male inmates and 179 female inmates in Special Housing Units.

[60]As part of our review on BOP's Special Management Units and Special Housing Units, we are analyzing their effects on inmate misconduct. We expect to publish our results in early 2013.

[61]New York State Department of Correctional Services, *Prison Safety in New York* (Albany, New York: April 2006).

officials have expanded inmates' program options. Officials from all five of the states we selected reported similar activities. Generally GED classes are held during the day, but, for example, two BOP facilities we visited have begun offering evening GED classes to accommodate the increase in inmates who are required to receive a GED education.[62] Also, one BOP facility we visited had expanded its vocational training capacity by combining woodshop learning with classroom study, so that one group of inmates could be learning in the woodshop while another group of inmates could be participating in classroom lessons. According to the program director, when he ran the program from 2001 through 2005, about 30 inmates received certification each year for completing the program; currently, about 60 to 80 inmates receive certification annually. At one facility we visited, to encourage program participation, inmates in the Special Management Unit were given cash incentives for completing psycho-educational programs, such as stress/anger management classes or those designed to improve interpersonal relationships and help inmates focus on personal goals and maintaining positive conduct. Specifically, an inmate may earn $25 for completing these types of classes.[63] Like BOP, both Ohio and Wisconsin have offered additional programming in the form of expanded program hours and expanded reentry programs; for example, classes on financial literacy, housing, and personal health care to teach inmates who are about to be released how to manage their daily lives in the community.

Efforts to Utilize Resources Efficiently

BOP's Federal Correctional Complex in Florence, Colorado, comprises three secure facilities: an Administrative Maximum U.S. Penitentiary, a high security U.S. Penitentiary, and a medium security Federal Correctional Institution. The complex also includes a minimum security satellite camp

Correctional complexes. BOP has established correctional complexes over the last 15 years to better leverage its staff. Officials from one state in our sample—Kansas—told us they employ this practice as well. BOP correctional complexes are institutions that are located on the same grounds and may include low, medium, and high security facilities. According to BOP officials, the use of correctional complexes helps in particular with the leveraging of medical services and supplies. It also

---

[62]According to BOP Program Statement 5350.28, generally an inmate confined in a federal institution who does not have a verified GED credential or high school diploma is required to attend an adult literacy program for a minimum of 240 instructional hours or until a GED is achieved, whichever occurs first.

[63]This program is funded by the BOP Inmate Trust Fund, which is maintained by profits from inmate purchases of commissary products, telephone services, and the fees inmates pay for using the inmate computer system. See GAO, *Bureau of Prisons: Improved Evaluations and Increased Coordination Could Improve Cell Phone Detection,* GAO-11-893 (Washington, D.C.: Sept. 6, 2011).

GAO-12-743 Federal Prison Crowding

helps BOP manage crowding by sharing staff resources across the correctional complex, if one facility has greater needs than another for certain programs.

Energy conservation. BOP has also taken actions to minimize the burden that crowding places on facilities' infrastructure, and officials from one state in our sample—Ohio—acknowledged similar activities. According to BOP officials, BOP has aggressively pursued energy conservation following a 2009 governmentwide executive order to reduce energy usage.[64] BOP officials stated that their energy-saving efforts have prevented BOP from experiencing a dramatic increase in energy usage despite the growing prison population. Examples of energy-saving actions that BOP officials reported include the installation of slower-flowing shower heads, which use 2 rather than 5 gallons of water per minute and flushing toilets every 5 to10 minutes rather than after each use. According to BOP officials, most BOP facilities have recycling programs. One BOP facility that we visited began a recycling program that, in addition to efficiently utilizing resources, created inmate jobs and benefitted the environment. Ohio officials told us that they have reduced utility costs with similar efficiency initiatives.

Visitor accommodations. BOP has taken a variety of actions to accommodate the increased number of visitors within existing infrastructure, which is similar to the steps officials from two of the five states we reviewed. For example, at one BOP facility we visited, because the facility did not have money to enlarge the visiting room, it shortened the length of visits from 4 hours to 2 hours and changed visiting hours from an open schedule (i.e., where visitors can come during any visiting hours) to a rotating basis (i.e., visitors for a particular inmate may be allowed to visit on certain days and between certain hours). In an effort to supplement face-to-face visits, BOP has permitted the increased use of e-mail between inmates and their loved ones.[65] Ohio and Wisconsin have implemented scheduled visitation times rather than open visitation hours.

---

[64]Federal Leadership in Environmental, Energy, and Economic Performance, Exec. Order No. 13514, 74 Fed. Reg. 52,117 (Oct. 5, 2009).

[65]An inmate is permitted to exchange electronic messages only with persons who have accepted the inmate's request to communicate. For more information on BOP's use of electronic messaging, see GAO-11-893.

In addition, Ohio officials told us that the state offers e-mail as a way to supplement visitation.

States Have Taken Broader Actions Intended to Reduce Prison Populations than Those Taken at the Federal Level

While BOP and the five selected states have taken a variety of similar actions to manage the growing number of inmates they incarcerate, these states have been able to take broader actions than BOP to reduce their prison populations because these states have legislative authority that BOP does not have.[66] These states' actions can be grouped into three general categories:

- modifying criminal statutes and sentencing,

- relocating inmates (e.g., moving them from state to local facilities or community corrections, whereby their release is supervised at halfway houses or in-home detention), or

- providing inmates with good time credit or adjusting inmates' sentences based on participation in certain programs or demonstration of positive behaviors.

To take these actions, these state departments of corrections have generally worked with their state legislatures to propose and pass legislation that effects these changes. Officials from three of the five states we spoke with—Kansas, Ohio, and Wisconsin—told us their states also embarked on justice reinvestment efforts to facilitate legislative or other changes to their corrections approaches.[67] For example, in 2006, Kansas sought technical assistance through the Justice Reinvestment

---

[66]Actions taken by states and discussed in this section have been intended to reduce prison populations. However, a variety of factors and circumstances (e.g., new drug sentencing laws and a drop in drug-related crime) may also have contributed to decreases in prison populations.

[67]The Justice Reinvestment Initiative is administered by DOJ's Bureau of Justice Assistance, Office of Justice Programs, in coordination with related efforts supported by independent organizations (e.g., the Pew Center on the States). It provides technical assistance and competitive financial support to states and localities engaged in or well positioned to consider different investments in their justice and law enforcement dollars. When considering reinvestment, states and localities collect and analyze data on drivers of criminal justice populations and costs, identify and implement changes to increase efficiencies, and measure both the fiscal and public safety impacts of any changes. Wisconsin participated in the initiative in 2008, but was no longer participating in the initiative at the time of our review.

Initiative to avert an increase of 700 new inmates in its prison population that it projected between 2007 and 2010. Using the justice reinvestment approach, as described below, Kansas (1) relocated inmates from state-run facilities by diverting them to nonprison alternatives and transferring them to county jails and community corrections facilities and (2) offered inmates credit for positive behavior thereby reducing inmates' time in prison. As a result, the state experienced a net increase of 10 inmates rather than the 700 inmates it had anticipated during this period.

Officials in the five selected states generally believed that the actions taken had helped them to reduce their prison populations; however, because these initiatives were recent, empirical data showing the impact of these initiatives were generally not available. In contrast, federal law does not provide BOP with the authority to implement many of these measures and generally requires BOP to provide for suitable housing and the safekeeping, care, and subsistence of all persons charged with or convicted of offenses against the United States.[68] Unlike certain states' laws, federal law does not provide BOP with the authority to transfer inmates to local prisons or move inmates to community corrections or supervised release beyond what current federal law permits.[69] Additionally, because of the mandatory minimum sentences required for many federal offenses and the absence of parole for most federal inmates in the federal system, BOP generally does not have the authority to significantly modify an inmate's period of incarceration.[70]

Modifying Criminal Statutes and Sentencing

Two of the five states we reviewed have changed their sentencing statutes or guidelines. For example, in 2009, New York implemented

---

[68]18 U.S.C. § 4042(a)(2). See GAO-12-320.

[69]The Second Chance Act of 2007, Pub. L. No. 110-199, § 251(a), 122 Stat. 657, 692-93, amended 18 U.S.C. § 3624(c) to enable BOP to place inmates in community corrections for up to 12 months and home detention for the shorter of 10 percent of the term of imprisonment or 6 months.

[70]According to the U.S. Parole Commission, offenders who are under the supervision of the commission and eligible for parole include inmates currently incarcerated for federal offenses committed prior to the Sentencing Reform Act of 1984; all District of Columbia offenders, as of August 5, 2000; the U.S. military prison population that has been transferred to federal correctional institutions; a few cases of Americans who have committed a crime in a foreign country; and offenders in the federal witness protection program.

changes to its drug statutes, which affected the sentencing of some drug felony offenders. These changes included revising the ranges for state prison sentences by lowering the minimum sentence allowable for certain nonviolent drug felony offenders. New York has reported decreases in its total custody population since 1999, when the population reached 71,472 and drug offenders constituted 31.2 percent of this population. From the end of calendar year 2009 through 2011, New York reported a decrease in its total custody population from 58,378 to 55,090. This decrease included not only a decline in the number of drug offenders from 10,319 to 7,509 but also in the percentage of drug offenders in custody from 17.7 percent to 13.6 percent. In 2011, Ohio revised its sentencing laws to eliminate the differences between the penalties for crack and powder cocaine violations. Generally, the change provides for a uniform determination of the penalty for drug offenses based upon the amount of any type of cocaine (powder cocaine or any compound, mixture, preparation, or substance containing cocaine) an individual possesses. In effect, this change resulted in an increasing of the amount of crack needed to those of powder cocaine for lower-level offenses and a decreasing of the amounts of powder cocaine needed to crack levels for higher-level offenses.

While states may change their sentencing statutes or guidelines to reduce their prison populations, at the federal level, BOP does not determine which offenders are sentenced to prison and what the length of their sentences should be. On May 1, 2007, the U.S. Sentencing Commission submitted to Congress amendments to the federal sentencing guidelines.[71] These guidelines became effective on November 1, 2007.[72] One of the amendments modified the drug quantity thresholds for crack

---

[71]Under 28 U.S.C. § 994(a), the commission is to promulgate and distribute to all of the courts of the United States and to the United States Probation System guidelines for use of a sentencing court in determining the sentence to be imposed in a criminal case, including (1) whether to impose a sentence to probation, a fine, or a term of imprisonment and (2) the appropriate amount of a fine or the length of a term of probation or imprisonment, among other things. Pursuant to 28 U.S.C. § 994(p), generally, the commission is to submit to Congress amendments to the guidelines and modifications to previously submitted amendments that have not taken effect.

[72]The federal sentencing guidelines provide federal judges with a set of consistent sentencing ranges to consult when determining a sentence. The guidelines consider both the seriousness of the criminal conduct and the defendant's criminal record. Federal courts must consult the sentencing guidelines and take them into account when sentencing, but are not bound to apply the guidelines.

GAO-12-743 Federal Prison Crowding

cocaine offenses. Generally, the commission lowered the sentencing guidelines for certain crack cocaine offenses. Subsequently, the commission made the amendment apply retroactively. As a result, some incarcerated offenders were eligible to receive a reduction in sentence under 18 U.S.C. § 3582(c)(2).[73] The effect of this change was realized almost fully in fiscal year 2008.[74]

Relocating Inmates

Selected states have also relocated inmates to relieve the crowding of their state prison facilities, such as through use of nonprison alternatives (e.g., drug treatment programs), expanded use of parole, the movement of inmates to county or local jails, or the wider reliance on community corrections (e.g., halfway houses). For example, Mississippi expanded use of house arrest and Kansas and New York expanded drug rehabilitation programs as an alternative to incarceration for certain low-level drug offenders. Other selected states have passed legislation that allows some inmates to be paroled sooner and made parole available to more inmates. For example, Mississippi has passed legislation that extended parole eligibility to (1) all nonviolent offenders irrespective of the offender's first-time offender status and (2) certain drug sale offenders. New York allows well-behaved drug and other nonviolent offenders to appear before a parole board earlier. Additionally, Kansas and Wisconsin have moved some low-risk inmates to county jails for more localized management and relief for state prison crowding.

Three of the five selected states also reported using community corrections—also known as supervised release at halfway houses or in-home detention—as a way to either divert offenders from prison or move more inmates out of prison. For example, Ohio uses halfway houses, as is typical, to provide supervision and treatment services to inmates who are released from state prison or are sentenced to halfway houses by

---

[73]See GAO-12-320.

[74]The change to the sentencing guidelines for crack cocaine went into effect on November 1, 2007. As of June 2011, the Sentencing Commission reported that of the 25,736 inmate applicants for a sentence reduction, 16,511 (64.2 percent) had been granted their requests. Eligible inmates received an average sentence reduction of 26 months. The Sentencing Commission was able to determine the origin of the motion for 15,016 of the inmates who were granted a sentence reduction. U.S. Sentencing Commission, *U.S. Sentencing Commission Preliminary Crack Cocaine Retroactivity Data Report, June 2011* (Washington, D.C.: June 2011).

courts for an offense or as a result of violating parole.[75] Like Ohio, Kansas has diverted parole and probation violators to supervised release. Similarly, Mississippi uses an intensive supervised release program as an alternative to incarceration for low-risk and nonviolent offenders.

At the federal level, BOP uses Residential Reentry Centers (RRC) to help inmates reintegrate into the community, as well as to reduce crowding in prisons, but is limited by what federal law allows as well as the capacity of these facilities.[76] BOP may place inmates there in the final months of their sentences (not to exceed 12 months) under conditions that will afford the inmate a reasonable opportunity to adjust to and prepare for reentry into the community. BOP officials stated that BOP maximizes the use of RRCs to the extent possible but that there are not enough beds in RRCs to accommodate all eligible inmates. In February 2012, we reported that as of November 2011, BOP estimated 8,859 available RRC beds under contract.[77] For each available RRC bed, BOP can transfer one inmate to the RRC for a maximum of 12 months, or BOP could send multiple inmates for shorter placements (e.g., three inmates for 4 months each). To provide all eligible inmates with the maximum allowable 12 months in an RRC, BOP would require about 29,000 available beds annually.[78] Further, BOP places inmates according to a court's or judge's sentence, which may require some probation and supervised release violators to serve terms in community corrections.

Providing Inmates with Credit for Positive Behaviors

Selected states have taken a variety of actions that reduce inmates' time in prison by providing inmates with credit for positive behaviors. For example, in Mississippi, certain inmates may be eligible to receive a trusty time allowance of 30 days' reduction of sentence for each 30 days' participation during any calendar month in approved programs while in

---

[75]In Ohio, generally parole is used for inmates convicted of crimes prior to July 1, 1996, when Ohio was under an indefinite sentencing structure. Most offenders who committed crimes after July 1, 1996, serve definite sentences, with a period of postrelease supervision for certain crimes upon their release from prison.

[76]BOP refers to halfway houses as RRCs.

[77]GAO-12-320.

[78]GAO, *Federal Bureau of Prisons: Methods for Estimating Incarceration and Community Corrections Costs and Results of the Elderly Offender Pilot*, GAO-12-807R (Washington, D.C.: Jul. 27, 2012).

trusty status.[79] According to Mississippi officials, these programs include alcohol and drug treatment, GED classes, faith-based programs, and vocational education. New York and Kansas allow inmates who complete certain rehabilitative programs to be released earlier, either through earned compliance credits in Kansas or by receiving a parole hearing earlier in New York. New York officials stated that since 1998, approximately 37,000 inmates have been released because of this policy. Ohio has an earned credit program that rewards an inmate for productive participation in educational programs, vocational training, prison industries work, substance abuse treatment, or any other constructive program with specific performance standards.[80] Additionally, in Ohio, there is a mechanism for the possible release with sentencing court approval of certain department of corrections inmates who have served at least 80 percent of their prison terms.[81]

Officials from two of the five selected states also reported that their states award inmates credit toward the service of their sentence for good behavior—compliance with institutional disciplinary regulations—as a way to relieve prison crowding. For example, Kansas's department of corrections offers good time credits and is authorized to adopt rules and regulations providing for a system of good time calculations. The system provides circumstances under which an inmate may earn good time credits and for the forfeiture of earned credits.[82]

We have previously reported on BOP's use of its sentence reduction authority, noting that it is affected by both inmate eligibility and BOP

---

[79]Pursuant to Miss. Code Ann. § 47-5-138.1, a trusty time allowance is a reduction in sentence that may be granted in addition to any other administrative reduction in sentence to an offender in trusty status as defined by the classification board of the Department of Corrections. In this instance, "trusty" refers to those inmates who are eligible to receive an allowance of 30 days reduction of sentence for each 30 days of their participation during any calendar month in an approved program

[80]Ohio Rev. Code Ann. § 2967.193.

[81]Ohio Rev. Code Ann. § 2967.19.

[82]Pursuant to Kan. Stat. Ann. § 21-6821, generally, the good time credit, which can be earned by an inmate and subtracted from any sentence, is limited to 15 percent of the prison part of the sentence for a crime committed on or after July 1, 1993, and increased to 20 percent of the prison part of the sentence for certain crimes committed on or after January 1, 2008.

GAO-12-743 Federal Prison Crowding

capacity.[83] Specifically, BOP's RDAP offers sentence reductions of up to 1 year to inmates convicted of a nonviolent offense who successfully complete the program. BOP officials told us that they strive to maximize RDAP programs as a management tool to reduce recidivism and because of the program's ability to reduce an inmate's sentence. RDAP programs are full, however, and BOP cannot keep up with demand for RDAP enrollment, which limits BOP's ability to fully leverage this program. Additionally, because of long waiting lists, those eligible for a sentence reduction are generally unable to complete RDAP in time to earn the maximum reduction. Furthermore, federal law provides for the amount of time awarded for each inmate who successfully completes the program. Moreover, according to BOP officials, given BOP's staffing shortages and in the absence of additional funding for the program, BOP has generally been unable to increase the number of RDAP's staff to accommodate more inmates.

Further, as we reported in February 2012, BOP is authorized to award up to 54 days of good conduct time credit each year (which vests on the date the inmate is released).[84] Good conduct time credit may be given to an inmate serving a sentence of more than 1 year, but less than life. BOP's method of awarding good conduct time credit at the end of each year an inmate serves results in a maximum of 47 days earned per year of sentence imposed.[85] From fiscal years 2009 through 2011, BOP data show that about 87 percent of inmates had earned all of their available good conduct time credit by the end of each year, and an additional 3 percent of inmates earned at least 90 percent of the maximum available good conduct time credit.[86]

Some inmates have contested BOP's methodology in court, maintaining that allowing inmates 54 days per year of sentence imposed was the

---

[83]GAO-12-320.

[84]GAO-12-320.

[85]As authorized in statute, 18 U.S.C. § 3624(b), BOP awards "up to 54 days at the end of each year of the prisoner's term of imprisonment," or 54 days per year of sentence served. As applied by BOP, this results in 47 days earned per year of sentence imposed because inmates do not earn good conduct time for years they do not ultimately serve because of being released early.

[86]BOP tracks inmates' earned good conduct time credit throughout their terms of imprisonment.

original intent of the statute,[87] but the U.S. Supreme Court upheld BOP's approach. BOP officials told us that the agency was supportive of amending the statute related to good conduct time credit, and legislation pending before Congress would allow for 54 days to be provided for each year of the term of imprisonment originally imposed by the judge, which would result in inmates serving 85 percent of their sentence.[88] BOP provided us with estimates in December 2011 showing that if the good conduct time credit allowance was increased from 47 to 54 days, as proposed, BOP could save over $40 million in the first fiscal year after the policy change from the early release of about 3,900 inmates. As of July 2012, the legislative proposal has been introduced in the Senate but not the House.[89] BOP officials told us that they are examining initiatives that would allow for the restoration of good conduct time, but that they are reluctant to pursue them. They explained that loss of good conduct time is one of the most powerful sanctions in BOP's inmate discipline program, which helps ensure the safety, security, and orderly operation of correctional facilities.

Concluding Observations

Over the last 25 years, BOP's population has grown more than 400 percent, and BOP projects future growth through 2020. With more inmates, BOP's spending to secure, feed, and provide services to a growing population has also been rising. BOP's annual appropriation now exceeds $6.6 billion, and represents nearly a quarter of DOJ's annual budgetary authority. Despite the continued growth in inmates and related expenses, in recent years, BOP has been adding capacity and staff at a lower rate than the inmate population has been growing. As a result, both

---

[87]Under the Sentencing Reform Act, the U.S. Sentencing Commission established sentencing guidelines with the understanding that inmates would receive good conduct time credit so that their actual time served would be 85 percent of the length of the sentence imposed by the judge, assuming good behavior. BOP's method of awarding good conduct time, however, results in inmates serving more than 85 percent of their imposed sentences, even after earning the maximum good conduct time credit.

[88]The additional credit would be awarded retroactively to inmates sentenced under the Sentencing Reform Act prior to the legislative change. For the hypothetical inmate with a 10-year sentence, the inmate would receive a total of 540 days of good conduct time. Thus the inmate would serve 3,110 days (85 percent) of the 3,650 days sentence.

[89]Second Chance Reauthorization Act of 2011, S.1231, 112th Cong. § 4(f) proposes to amend certain statutory provisions related to good conduct time in 18 U.S.C. § 3624(b)(1). As of August 2012, the legislative proposal has been introduced in the Senate but not the House.

individual facilities and the federal prison system as a whole are experiencing increased crowding. Crowding has implications for inmates, staff, and infrastructure—as well as safety and security, and the potential for inmate disruptions or an even more serious security incident is a significant concern. BOP has taken steps to help mitigate the implications of crowding in the federal system, but does not have the authority to implement many of the reforms that several states have adopted to reduce crowding and, in some states, the size of their prison populations. BOP also requires congressional approval and appropriated funds to expand capacity in the federal system. As such, BOP has limited ability to address crowding in the federal prison system. We are not taking a position on matters of policy such as how crowding in the federal system should be addressed. However, as policy makers weigh whether and how to address crowding in the federal system, options that will be important to consider include (1) reducing the size of the projected inmate population by reforming sentencing laws, allowing alternatives to incarceration, and/or providing BOP greater sentencing flexibility; (2) increasing capacity in the federal system by constructing new prisons, contracting for additional private capacity, and adding additional staff; or (3) taking some combination of both approaches.

Agency Comments

We provided a draft of this report to DOJ for official review and comment. BOP provided technical clarifications, which we incorporated where appropriate.

We are sending copies of this report to the Attorney General, selected congressional committees, and other interested parties. In addition, this report is available at no charge on the GAO website at http://www.gao.gov.

If you or your staff have any further questions about this report, please contact me at (202) 512-9627 or maurerd@gao.gov. Contact points for our Offices of Congressional Relations and Public Affairs may be found on the last page of this report. Key contributors to this report are listed in appendix IV.

David C. Maurer
Director
Homeland Security and Justice

Appendix I: Objectives, Scope, and Methodology

Our objectives for this report were to address the following questions:

1. What was the growth in the Bureau of Prison's (BOP) population from fiscal years 2006 through 2011, and what are BOP's projections for inmate population and capacity?

2. What is known about the effects of a growing federal prison population on operations (i.e., inmates, staff, and infrastructure) within BOP facilities, and to what extent has BOP taken actions to mitigate these effects?

3. What actions have selected states taken to reduce their prison populations, and to what extent has BOP implemented similar initiatives?

To address the first question, we analyzed BOP's statutory authority and policies and procedures (e.g., BOP's inmate classification policy) that potentially affect growth in the federal prison population and conditions of confinement in BOP facilities. We also analyzed BOP's (1) inmate population data (e.g., demographics and offenses), (2) 2020 long-range capacity plan based on inmate population projections and future capacity estimates depending on funding,[1] (3) percentage crowding at all institutional security levels, (4) staff-to-inmate ratios, and (5) available infrastructure costs (e.g., water and electricity costs). Unless otherwise noted, all of these data covered the period from fiscal years 2006 through 2011. We also reviewed Department of Justice (DOJ) and BOP reports describing BOP's population and staffing during this period. We assessed the reliability of BOP's inmate population data and crowding data by reviewing relevant documentation, interviewing knowledgeable agency officials about how they maintain the integrity of their data, and updating assessments that we did for previously issued reports. We found BOP's inmate population and crowding data to be sufficiently reliable for the purposes of this engagement.

To determine how BOP developed its population and capacity projection estimates, we analyzed BOP's program statements, performance goals, and congressional budget submissions for fiscal years 2011 through 2013. We also interviewed BOP headquarters officials to discuss the extent to which BOP's population has grown; the reasons for this growth; how BOP

---

[1]We analyzed BOP's 2020 long-range capacity plan dated January 10, 2012.

GAO-12-743 Federal Prison Crowding

calculates the percentage crowding in its facilities; and how BOP develops its population growth and capacity projections, including any changes to this process since our November 2009 report.[2] In that report, we assessed how BOP developed its population projections and capacity plans. We compared BOP's projections with its actual inmate population growth from fiscal years 1999 through August 20, 2009, and concluded that BOP's projections were accurate, on average, to within 1 percent of the actual inmate population growth within this time period. We also reviewed government and academic studies on federal incarceration determinants.

To address the second question, we analyzed BOP's statutory authority, policies, and procedures pertinent to the effects of the growing prison population on BOP operations, including inmates, staff, and infrastructure, and that may affect BOP's ability to mitigate the effects of a growing population. Further, we analyzed BOP studies on the effects of population growth and crowding on BOP operations. We also analyzed data provided by BOP on available bed space including temporary bed space for all security levels,[3] inmate program participation and waiting lists, inmate-to-staff ratios, and available infrastructure costs. Unless otherwise noted, these data covered the period from fiscal years 2006 through 2011. We also present systemwide BOP staffing ratios from fiscal years 1997 through 2011 because officials believed that presenting the ratios for a longer period better illustrates the effect of BOP's population growth relative to the number of staff.[4] We assessed the reliability of BOP's inmate, staff, and infrastructure data by interviewing knowledgeable agency officials to determine how BOP collects and maintains the integrity of these data. We found these data to be sufficiently reliable for the purposes of this report. In addition, we reviewed BOP's fiscal year 2011 congressional budget submission to identify past actions to address federal prison population growth and crowding, including any proposed legislative changes. To observe some of the effects of a growing federal prison population and crowding on current BOP inmates, staff, and

---

[2]See GAO-10-94.

[3]BOP reports the use of additional cots in areas such as an institution's halls, gyms, mezzanines, or television rooms—to address crowding in an institution—as temporary housing because this temporary living space is to be restored as program space when circumstances permit. Thus, such temporary use of space is not factored into BOP's rated capacity calculation.

[4]According to BOP officials, BOP also includes this information in its annual congressional budget request.

infrastructure, we conducted visits to 5 of BOP's 117 institutions. We chose these prisons on the basis of varying security levels and to ensure geographic dispersion. As shown in table 1, the five prisons we visited were located in four of BOP's six regions. Additionally, to identify variations in the effects of increased prison populations, we selected facilities of different security levels (i.e., low, 1; medium, 3; high, 1; and administrative, 1); the Petersburg Complex included a medium and a low security facility.

Table 1: Site Visits to BOP Facilities

Facility name	Region	Security level
Petersburg Complex	Mid-Atlantic Region	Low, medium
SeaTac	Western Region	Administrative—mixed security levels including men and women
Lewisburg	Northeast Region	High, Special Management Unit
Schuylkill	Northeast Region	Medium
Leavenworth	North Central Region	Medium (previously high)

Source: GAO analysis of BOP information.

During each site visit, we interviewed institutional management officials and toured the facility to observe inmate housing, recreational areas, food service, medical services, and educational and vocational programming. Because we did not visit all BOP facilities and did not randomly select the facilities we visited, our results are not generalizable to all BOP facilities. Nevertheless, these results provided us with examples of the effects of BOP's population growth on a facility's inmates, staff, and infrastructure, as well as examples of actions taken at the facility level to mitigate these effects. We also interviewed the six regional directors to obtain their perspectives on the increased prison population and the effects of this growth and crowding on BOP institutions within each region. Further, we discussed the effects of BOP's population growth on correctional officers with officials from the Council of Prison Locals, the union that represents all non-management staff working in BOP facilities. Additionally, we analyzed American Correctional Association's (ACA) standards (e.g., minimum inmate space standards) and reviewed ACA audits from fiscal years 2009 through 2011 (the most recent audits available) of the BOP institutions we visited to try to identify potential effects of growing

populations in these facilities. We also met with ACA officials to identify
any areas where BOP might not be meeting these standards.[5]

Further, to determine the extent to which BOP has taken actions to mitigate
the effects of a growing federal prison population, we analyzed BOP's
statutory authority to identify provisions that affect BOP's ability to mitigate
the effects of the growth of the prison population. We also analyzed BOP's
policies, DOJ and BOP studies, and BOP's fiscal year 2011 congressional
budget submission to identify actions BOP has taken, including any
proposed legislative changes that could mitigate the effects of the growth of
the prison population. We interviewed BOP headquarters officials to obtain
information on these actions and proposals as well as to discuss the extent
of their statutory authority, which affects their ability to mitigate the effects
of the increased population. During our BOP site visits and interviews with
BOP regional directors, we asked officials to identify any actions taken at
the facility or regional level to mitigate the effects of the growth of the
federal prison population and crowding in facilities in the region. Also, we
discussed actions taken by BOP to mitigate the effects of prison population
growth with officials from the Council of Prison Locals. We also interviewed
corrections experts from DOJ's National Institute of Corrections (NIC),[6]
ACA, Pew Center on the States, and academia. We selected these experts
from our review of the corrections literature and on the recommendation of
BOP officials and other experts. While the views of these experts are not
representative, they provided us with perspectives on BOP's actions and
ability to mitigate the effects of its increased prison population.

To also address the second as well as the third questions, we compared
and contrasted BOP's actions to (1) mitigate the effects of its increased
population and (2) attempt to reduce its prison population with similar
actions taken by five states—Kansas, Mississippi, New York, Ohio, and

---

[5]ACA's mission includes the development and promotion of effective standards for the
care, custody, training, and treatment of offenders. As part of its accreditation process, a
visiting committee of ACA auditors (1) audits the corrections agency or correctional facility
against standards and expected practices documentation and (2) evaluates the quality of
life or conditions of confinement. An acceptable quality of life is necessary for an agency
to be eligible for accreditation. The quality of life in a facility includes staff training, cell size
and time inmates spend outside the cells, current population, adequacy of medical
services, offender programs, recreation, food service, classification, sanitation, use of
segregation, crowding, and reported and/or documentation of incidents of violence.

[6]NIC, a component of BOP, provides training, technical assistance, information services, and
policy/program development assistance to federal, state, and local corrections agencies.

Wisconsin—that had experienced prison population growth and had
taken actions to mitigate its effects or reduce their prison populations. To
select these states, we analyzed DOJ's Bureau of Justice Statistics's
(BJS) report on 2010 state prison inmate populations.[7] We also reviewed
relevant governmental and nongovernmental reports on state prison
population growth and states' actions taken to reduce or mitigate the
effects this growth, which were published from 2006 through 2011 (e.g.,
the Pew Center on the States, Vera Institute, and Council of State
Governments). We also interviewed (1) BOP, NIC, and BJS officials; (2)
stakeholder interest groups (e.g., Pew Center on the States, Council of
State Governments, ACA, and Association of State Correctional
Administrators); and (3) academic corrections experts to obtain their
perspectives on state efforts to mitigate the effects of prison population
growth or reduce prison populations.

We selected these five states because they (1) reflected a range of prison
population sizes (e.g., New York and Ohio have two of the largest state
prison populations, with 56,656 and 51,712 inmates, respectively); (2)
were involved in addressing prison crowding issues (e.g., Kansas and
Ohio are working with the Council of State Governments and the Pew
Center on the States to address prison crowding issues as part of the
Justice Reinvestment Initiative); and (3) had taken actions to address
population growth, including actions similar to BOP's actions.[8]

For each of the five selected states, we obtained available data (e.g., BJS
state correctional population) and reviewed relevant studies on prison
conditions for context. We then interviewed state corrections officials

---

[7]See BJS, *Prisoners in 2010* (Washington, D.C.: December 2011) and *Prisoners in 2009*
(Washington, D.C. December 2010). BJS is the statistical agency of DOJ.

[8]The Justice Reinvestment Initiative, which is administered by DOJ's Bureau of Justice
Assistance in the Office of Justice Programs in coordination with related efforts supported
by independent organizations (e.g., the Pew Center on the States), provides technical
assistance and competitive financial support to states and localities engaged in or well
positioned to undertake justice reinvestment. The purpose of justice reinvestment is to
manage and allocate criminal justice populations more cost-effectively, generating savings
that can be reinvested in evidence-based strategies that increase public safety while
holding offenders accountable. States and localities engaging in Justice Reinvestment
Initiative activities collect and analyze data on drivers of criminal justice populations and
costs, identify and implement changes to increase efficiencies, and measure both the
fiscal and public safety impacts of those changes. According to Wisconsin officials,
Wisconsin participated in the initiative in 2008, but was no longer participating in the
initiative at the time of our review.

regarding actions taken in their states to reduce the prison population, as
well as to mitigate the effects of prison population growth. We analyzed
correctional statutes and policies identified by these officials during our
interviews. As shown in table 2, we also conducted site visits to three
facilities in two states.

Table 2: Site Visits to State Correctional Facilities

State	Facility name	Security level
Kansas	Lansing	Maximum, medium, and minimum
New York	Edgecombe	Low (parole violators; substance abuse)
New York	Sing Sing	Maximum

Source: GAO, based on state data.

During our site visits, we discussed with correctional administrators and
observed actions taken within these facilities to mitigate the effects of the
growth of the prison populations.

Additionally, to further address the third question, we assessed the extent
to which actions implemented in the five states to reduce their prison
populations would be possible under current federal law for BOP to
implement. Dissimilarities between federal and state prison systems—
legally, structurally, and in how crowding calculations are determined—
limit the comparability between federal and state correctional systems.
We mitigated the effects of these limitations by the criteria used to select
the five states. We are unable to generalize about the types of actions
states have taken to mitigate the effects of state prison population growth
or reduce their prison populations. Nevertheless, the information we
obtained through these visits provided examples of state responses to
prison population growth. Further, to determine the extent to which BOP
has implemented similar initiatives from states' experiences, we analyzed
BOP documentation describing BOP initiatives to address the growth of
federal prison populations. We also discussed with BOP officials the state
actions we identified, including the extent to which these actions would be
possible under current federal law for BOP to implement.

We conducted this performance audit from September 2011 to
September 2012 in accordance with generally accepted government
auditing standards. Those standards require that we plan and perform the
audit to obtain sufficient, appropriate evidence to provide a reasonable
basis for our findings and conclusions based on our audit objectives. We
believe that the evidence obtained provides a reasonable basis for our
findings and conclusions based on our audit objectives.

Appendix II: BOP's Population Growth

This appendix presents additional information and elaboration on BOP's population growth. Specifically, it addresses

- factors contributing to growth,

- offense composition of BOP's population,

- BOP's rated capacity and percentage crowding trends, and

- BOP's long-range capacity plan.

Factors Contributing to Growth

Among the factors that contribute to the size of the federal prison population are national crime levels, law enforcement policies, and federal sentencing laws, all of which are beyond BOP's control. According to BOP officials, the length of the sentences that federal inmates serve is one of the single most important factors in prison population growth. Prior to the passage of the Sentencing Reform Act of 1984, most federal statutes provided only for broad maximum terms of imprisonment and federal judges had broad discretion in sentencing.[1] Federal law outlined the maximum sentence, federal judges imposed a sentence within a statutory range, and federal parole officials eventually determined the actual duration of incarceration. The Sentencing Reform Act of 1984 abolished parole, and subsequent legislation established mandatory minimum sentences for many federal offenses; these federal laws limit the ability of BOP to affect the length of the sentence or the size of the inmate population.

According to BOP, the increase in sentence length is the primary reason for the growth in the federal inmate population from 42,000 in 1987 to over 218,000 today. Drug offenses constitute the largest component of admissions to BOP. The average time an inmate served for drug offenses increased 250 percent after 1987, when the U.S. Sentencing Commission revised the U.S. Sentencing Guidelines in order to implement the

---

[1]The Sentencing Reform Act of 1984, Pub. L. No 98-473, 98 Stat. 1987, changed the federal sentencing structure. The act was effective for offenses committed on or after November 1, 1987.

Sentencing Reform Act of 1984.[2] Most recently, the Administrative Office of the U. S. Courts reported to BOP that for the year ending March 31, 2012, federal courts had ordered over 8,000 sentences of 6 or more years, and nearly 3,000 of those prison sentences were for 12 or more years.[3] Beyond drug offenses, BOP reported that length of sentence for almost all federal offenders had increased since the implementation of the act. For example, immigration offenders currently serve much longer sentences than they did in the 1980s.

Offense Composition of BOP's Population

As shown in table 3, drug, weapons/explosives, and immigration offenses composed the largest number of offenses for which all BOP inmates were incarcerated in each year from fiscal years 2006 through 2011.[4]

---

[2]The U.S. Sentencing Commission is an independent agency in the judicial branch of government. Its principal purposes are (1) to establish sentencing policies and practices for the federal courts, including guidelines to be consulted regarding the appropriate form and severity of punishment for offenders convicted of federal crimes; (2) to advise and assist Congress and the executive branch in the development of effective and efficient crime policy; and (3) to collect, analyze, research, and distribute a broad array of information on federal crime and sentencing issues.

[3]The Administrative Office of the U.S. Courts is the central support entity for the judicial branch. It provides a wide range of administrative, legal, financial, management, program, and information technology services to the federal courts.

[4]BOP officials explained that for reporting purposes they categorize inmates according to the offense for which an inmate is serving the longest sentence (dominant sentence offense). For example, an inmate may be serving sentences for both drug and immigration offenses, but BOP will categorize the inmate by the offense having the longer sentence (e.g., the drug offense).

Table 3: Offense Composition of the Inmate Population in BOP Facilities, by Year, from Fiscal Years 2006 through 2011

Offense	Fiscal year					
	2006	2007	2008	2009	2010	2011
Drugs	91,690	95,321	94,456	96,415	96,094	97,164
Weapons/explosives	27,036	28,901	30,256	31,454	32,188	33,136
Immigration	18,992	19,862	20,165	22,298	21,767	24,800
Fraud/bribery/extortion	8,426	9,268	10,229	10,493	10,930	11,462
Sex offenses	3,824	4,754	5,989	7,308	8,610	9,653
Robbery	9,428	9,099	8,965	8,712	8,493	8,289
Burglary/larceny	6,381	6,417	6,499	6,694	6,747	7,136
Homicide/aggravated assault	4,895	4,942	4,940	4,894	4,900	5,114
Court/corrections	2,174	2,209	2,192	2,180	2,183	2,200
Miscellaneous[a]	2,374	2,298	2,305	2,281	2,064	2,006
Counterfeiting/embezzlement	1,066	1,016	1,017	945	928	948
Continuing criminal enterprise[b]	430	416	412	390	374	364
National security	108	103	105	98	97	95
Total offender population	**176,824**	**184,606**	**187,530**	**194,162**	**195,375**	**202,367**

Source: GAO analysis of BOP data.

Notes: Sentencing information is not available for all inmates, for example, pretrial inmates whose information has not been entered into the data system.

[a]Miscellaneous offenses include criminal civil rights violations; food and drug violations; economic espionage; destruction of an energy facility; District of Columbia offenses, such as driving while intoxicated, malicious mischief, and contributing to the delinquency of a minor; and violations of fish and game laws.

[b]Continuing criminal enterprise refers to sentencing under the Racketeer Influenced and Corrupt Organizations Act (RICO) Act (codified at 18 U.S.C. § 1961), for example, drug kingpins.

BOP explained that the offense composition of BOP's population generally shows a higher number of drug offenses than immigration offenses, because drug offenses carry longer sentences than immigration offenses. For example, BOP data show that the number of drug offenses in fiscal year 2011 was four times greater than the number of immigration offenses that year, although the yearly admission to BOP for each of these offenses is usually about the same. Further, the number of admissions for weapons offenses is generally about one-fourth that of immigration offenses, but the number of weapons offenders in the BOP population is significantly higher than the number of immigration offenders because of the much longer sentences for weapons offenses.

The distribution of offenses varied by institutional security level, although, with the exception of high security facilities, drug violations constituted the largest number of offenses. In medium and low security facilities, drugs, weapons/explosives, and immigration were among the three largest offense categories. In minimum security facilities, drug offenses were followed by fraud/bribery/extortion and weapons/explosives offenses.[5] In high security facilities, weapons/explosives offenses constituted the largest number of offenses, followed by drugs, robbery, homicide/aggravated assault, and immigration.

As shown in table 4, drug and immigration offenses accounted for the largest numbers of offenses among non-U.S. citizen inmates in each year of the 6-year period. Violent and property offenses increased during the same period, but were a smaller number of the total offenses.

Table 4: Offense Composition of the Non-U.S. Citizen Inmate Population in BOP Facilities from Fiscal Years 2006 through 2011

Dominant offense	Year					
	2006	2007	2008	2009	2010	2011
Drug offenses	19,980	21,450	21,501	21,690	20,931	22,135
Immigration offenses	15,509	16,819	16,570	18,227	17,978	21,451
Violent offenses	1,908	2,086	2,288	2,387	2,481	2,696
Property offenses	1,047	1,190	1,470	1,423	1,429	1,532
Miscellaneous	1,505	1,615	1,656	1,621	1,655	1,746

Source: GAO analysis of BOP data.

Note: Drug offenses include the distribution of narcotics to a minor and possession of narcotics. Immigration offenses include illegal entry and illegal reentry into the United States. Violent offenses include assault, homicide, bank robbery, and firearms/weapons/explosive violations. Property offenses include embezzlement, auto theft, larceny, and destroying government property. Other offenses include sex offenses (e.g., obscene mailing and white slavery); justice system offenses (e.g., perjury, obstruction of justice, and jumping bail); racketeering; general offenses (e.g., bribery, extortion, and failure to pay child support); and regulatory offenses (e.g., customs law violations, espionage, sabotage, and violations of national defense laws), among other things.

During each year of the 6-year period, the largest number of non-U.S. citizen inmates (ranging from about 28,000 to 33,000) were incarcerated in low security facilities for drug offenses. Among non-U.S. citizen inmates incarcerated in medium and high security facilities, immigration, followed by drugs, constituted the largest number of offenses. As to why these inmates were housed in medium and high security facilities, BOP officials explained

---

[5]BOP does not send non-U.S. citizen inmates to minimum security facilities because of their risk of flight.

that offenders who were convicted of violent offenses, had a history of violent behavior, or had been found guilty of serious misconduct while in BOP custody were usually sent to higher security level facilities. These officials said that over 45 percent of non-U.S. citizen inmates who were placed in higher security level facilities had a history of violence.

BOP's Rated Capacity and Percentage Crowding Trends

Table 5 below shows BOP's rated capacity and double, triple, and quadruple bunking levels as of September 30, 2011.

Table 5: BOP's Rated Capacity and Crowding, by Facility Security Level as of September 2011

Facility type	Rated capacity	Actual population	Actual inmates double bunked		Actual inmates triple bunked		Actual inmates quadruple bunked	Percentage crowding
			Number	Percentage	Number	Percentage		
Male[a]								
Minimum	18,476	21,091	13,246	63%	7,845	37%	0	14%
Low	32,242	44,174	8,384	19%	35,790	81%	0	37%
Medium	41,039	61,908	40,338	65%	21,570	35%	0	51%
High[b]	13,570	20,978	20,244	97%	0	0%	0	55%
Female[c]								
Minimum	4,207	5,086	2,449	48%	2,637	52%	0	21%
Secure	3,808	5,866	0	0%	5,250	89%	616	54%

Source: GAO analysis of BOP data.

Notes: According to BOP, rated capacity is the maximum population level at which an institution can make available basic necessities, essential services (e.g., medical care), and programs (e.g., drug treatment, basic education, and vocational education). BOP calculates rated capacity only for the prisons that it operates; therefore, private institutions are excluded. Further, BOP does not calculate rated capacity for residential reentry centers or inmates in home confinement because BOP does not assign security levels to these confinement arrangements. The capacity figures used to calculate percentages and determine double and triple occupancy for this table are from BOP end of fiscal year 2011 historical information from BOP's 2020 long range capacity plan.

[a]Male long-term institutions include four security level designations—minimum, low, medium, and high.

[b]The remaining 3 percent of inmates in high security facilities are single-bunked.

[c]Female facilities include three security designations—high, secure, and minimum, but female high security facilities are single bunked.

As a result of the growth in the inmate population in BOP-run facilities relative to the increased rated capacity, crowding in BOP-run institutions increased from 36 to 39 percent systemwide from fiscal years 2006 through 2011. Nevertheless, within male facilities, the percentage crowding varied by security level, as shown in figure 4. For example, the percentage crowding in male medium security facilities increased from 37 percent to 51 percent, and from 53 percent to 55 percent in high security level facilities (see table 6). Additionally, the percentage crowding in minimum security facilities more than doubled from fiscal year 2009 through 2010 because of a population increase of more than 1,400 inmates while capacity increased by 69 beds.

Figure 4: Percentage Crowding in Male Long-Term Facilities from Fiscal Years 2006 through 2011 by Institutional Security Level

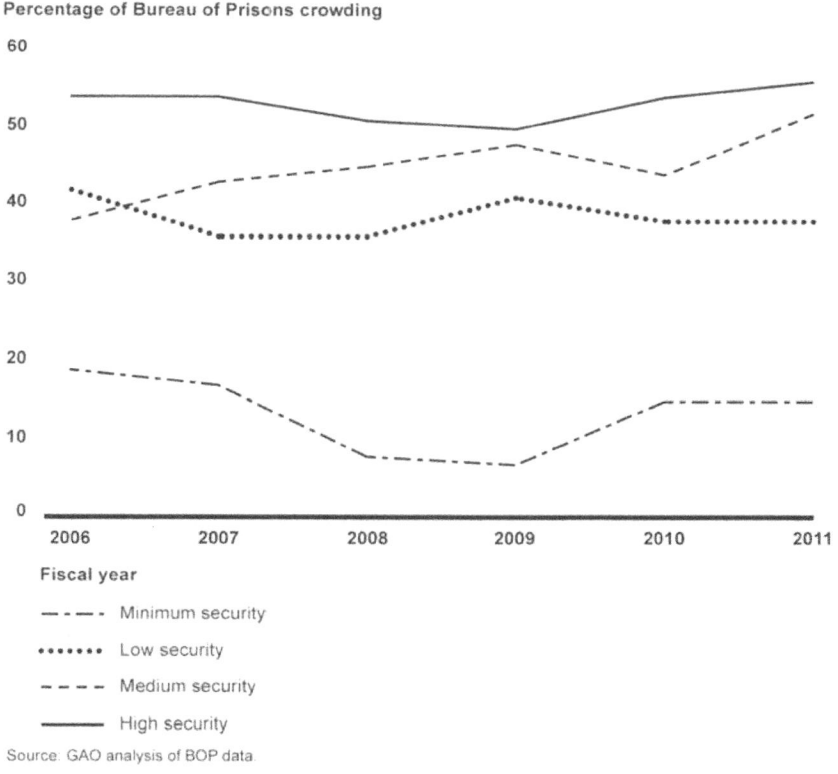

Percentage of Bureau of Prisons crowding

Fiscal year

— - — · Minimum security

······· Low security

— — — Medium security

——— High security

Source: GAO analysis of BOP data.

During the 6-year period, the overall percentage crowding in female long-term facilities decreased from 39 to 36 percent, but there were some variations by facility security level (i.e., minimum, secure, and high). Specifically, the percentage crowding in secure facilities decreased from 73 to 54 percent and the percentage crowding in minimum security facilities increased from 17 to 21 percent. BOP headquarters officials explained that BOP was able to increase the number of female secure facility beds by converting a male facility at Waseca, Minnesota, to a female facility.[6]

Table 6 shows BOP's male and female populations, rated capacity, and percentage crowding data by institutional security level for fiscal years 2006 through 2011.

---

[6]BOP officials explained that BOP was able to convert the male facility because it had opened a new male facility and converted older male high security facilities to medium security facilities, thereby increasing the number of beds available for male inmates.

Table 6: BOP Population, Rated Capacity, and Percentage Crowding from Fiscal Years 2006 through 2011

Security level of facility	2006			2007			2008			2009			2010			2011		
	Pop	Cap	%Cro	Pop	Cap	%Cro	Pop	Cap	%Cro	Pop	Cap	%Cro	Pop	Cap	%Cro	Pop	Cap	%Cro
Total inmates in BOP-run institutions	162,514	119,510	36%	167,323	122,189	37%	165,964	122,366	36%	172,423	125,778	37%	173,289	126,713	37%	177,934	127,795	39%
Males	151,003	111,067	36%	155,254	113,111	37%	153,992	113,288	36%	160,315	116,050	38%	161,295	117,171	38%	165,595	118,596	40%
Long-Term	133,331	97,439	37%	137,195	100,170	37%	136,138	100,361	36%	142,005	102,867	38%	143,059	104,003	38%	148,151	105,327	41%
Minimum	20,046	16,963	18%	20,003	17,271	16%	18,556	17,353	7%	18,904	17,768	6%	20,329	17,837	14%	21,091	18,476	14%
Low	43,723	31,037	41%	41,646	30,791	35%	41,825	31,081	35%	45,153	32,294	40%	44,264	32,302	37%	44,174	32,242	37%
Medium	51,972	37,911	37%	56,492	39,680	42%	55,543	38,479	44%	57,904	39,375	47%	57,708	40,294	43%	61,908	41,039	51%
High	17,590	11,528	53%	19,054	12,428	53%	20,214	13,448	50%	20,044	13,430	49%	20,758	13,570	53%	20,978	13,570	55%
Florence ADX[a]	462	490	-6%	476	490	-3%	476	490	-3%	458	490	-7%	444	490	-9%	451	490	-8%
Marion	0	804	0%	0	0	0%	0	0	0%	0	0	0%	0	0	0%	0	0	0%
Medical	2,715	2,646	3%	2,642	2,657	-1%	2,622	2,604	1%	2,683	2,604	3%	2,505	2,487	1%	2,501	2,517	-1%
Detention	14,085	9,349	51%	14,521	9,455	54%	14,335	9,494	51%	14,741	9,721	52%	14,877	9,823	51%	14,085	9,878	43%
Witness security[b]	410	339	21%	420	339	24%	421	339	24%	428	368	16%	410	368	11%	407	384	6%
Females	11,511	8,443	36%	12,069	9,078	33%	11,972	9,078	32%	12,108	9,728	24%	11,994	9,542	26%	12,339	9,199	34%
Long-Term	10,060	7,253	39%	10,691	7,847	36%	10,690	7,847	36%	10,730	8,497	26%	10,691	8,311	29%	10,971	8,039	36%
Minimum	5,192	4,429	17%	5,362	4,429	21%	5,134	4,429	16%	5,026	4,479	12%	5,003	4,479	12%	5,086	4,207	21%
Secure	4,853	2,800	73%	5,311	3,394	56%	5,537	3,394	63%	5,690	3,994	42%	5,671	3,808	49%	5,866	3,808	54%
High	15	24	-38%	18	24	-25%	19	24	-21%	14	24	-42%	17	24	-29%	19	24	-21%
Medical	393	378	4%	574	378	52%	466	378	23%	521	378	38%	481	378	27%	435	378	15%
Detention	1,058	812	30%	804	853	-6%	816	853	-4%	857	853	0%	822	853	-4%	933	782	19%

Legend:

Pop refers to inmate population.

Cap refers to rated capacity of the facility.

% Cro refers to the percentage crowding.

Source: BOP.

Notes: BOP designates some of its institutions as administrative institutions, which specifically serve inmates awaiting trial, or those with intensive medical or mental health conditions, regardless of the level of supervision these inmates require.

[a]The Administrative Maximum (ADX) facility in Florence, Colorado, houses offenders requiring the tightest controls.

[b]Witness security refers to BOP housing for inmates in the federal Witness Security Program.

BOP's 2020 Long-Range Capacity Plan

BOP's 2020 long-range capacity plan projects continued growth in the federal prison population from fiscal years 2012 through 2020.[1] The plan relies on multiple approaches to house the increased federal prison population, including contracting with the private sector for certain inmate populations; expanding existing institutions where infrastructure permits; and acquiring, constructing, and activating new facilities as funding permits. BOP officials explained that BOP changes its capacity plan several times each year. For example, rated capacity figures may change as a result of the reclassification of a facility to address population needs. BOP also adjusts its actual capacity and population figures each year.

As shown in figure 5, BOP expects the overall inmate population in BOP-run institutions to continue to grow from approximately 182,600 inmates in fiscal year 2012 to about 204,410 inmates in fiscal year 2020. The plan also projects an increase in systemwide capacity from 128,433 beds in 2012 to 151,895 beds in 2020, with a projected reduction in crowding from 42 percent to 35 percent.

[1]These projections are from BOP's 2020 capacity plan dated January 10, 2012. In November 2009, we concluded that BOP's projections were accurate, on average, to within 1 percent of the actual inmate population growth from fiscal year 1999 through August 20, 2009. See GAO-10-94.

Figure 5: BOP's Projections for Population, Rated Capacity, and Percentage Crowding from Fiscal Years 2012 through 2020

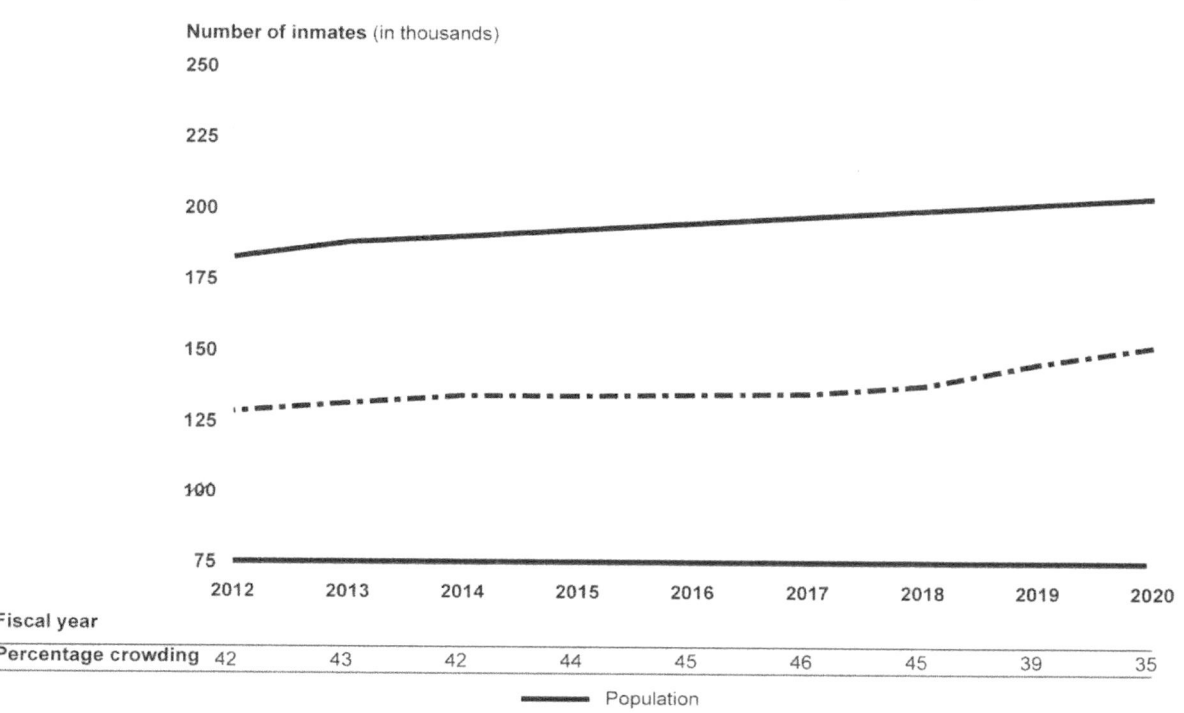

Fiscal year	2012	2013	2014	2015	2016	2017	2018	2019	2020
Percentage crowding	42	43	42	44	45	46	45	39	35

——— Population

■ ·■· Rated capacity

Source: GAO analysis of BOP data.

Specifically, BOP's 2020 capacity plan projects the male inmate populations in long-term institutions at all security levels to continue to grow or remain stable; however, BOP projects variations in the changes in rated capacity across the security levels, resulting in respective differences in crowding percentages. For example, as shown in figure 6, from fiscal years 2017 through 2020, BOP's plan projects a decrease in crowding in male medium security facilities from 71 percent to 58 percent and in high security facilities from 55 percent to 12 percent, as a result of the projected increased capacity.[2] Congressional budget requests have

---

[2]BOP's 2020 long-range capacity plan, dated January 10, 2012, projects an increased capacity of 5,808 (43,239 to 49,047) beds and increased population of 3,812 (73,737 to 77,549) inmates in male medium security facility between fiscal years 2017 and 2020. In male high security facilities, the plan projects an increased capacity of 7,200 (15,485 to 22,685) beds and increased population of 1,320 (24,012 to 25,332) inmates from fiscal years 2017 and 2020.

not included funding for this additional bed space, and as a result BOP's plans are contingent on the budget development and appropriations processes and are subject to change. During the same period, BOP also projects crowding in low security facilities to be about 35 percent.

Figure 6: Projected Percentage Crowding in Male Long-Term Facilities from Fiscal Years 2012 through 2020 by Security Level

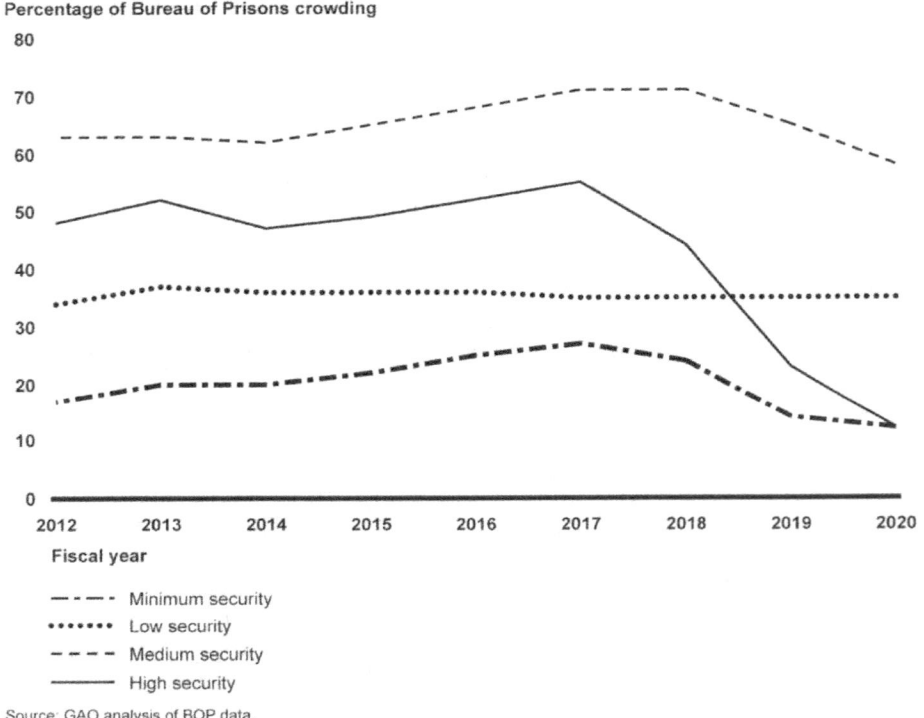

Percentage of Bureau of Prisons crowding

Fiscal year

— - — - Minimum security
••••••• Low security
— — — Medium security
———— High security

Source: GAO analysis of BOP data.

BOP's plan also projects an increase in the female long-term inmate population from fiscal years 2012 through 2020, but anticipates variations in percentage crowding across security levels. Specifically, the projections show an increase in the percentage crowding in female minimum security facilities from 24 to 37 percent and a decrease in the percentage crowding in female secure facilities from 58 to 32 percent. BOP noted that this reduction in crowding is contingent on appropriations to fund the opening of a secure female facility in Aliceville, Alabama, in fiscal years 2013 and 2014. According to BOP officials, BOP's projections do not include any additional long-term facilities for women, because the percentage crowding in female facilities is well below the percentage crowding in, for example, male medium security facilities. Nevertheless, officials said that BOP will review and adjust capacity needs as it develops its plan beyond fiscal year 2020.

Table 7 shows BOP's rated capacity, population, and percentage crowding projections from fiscal years 2012 through 2020. According to BOP officials, BOP's long-term population projections are always conservative; therefore, the actual number of inmates would likely be higher than the projections. Additionally, they said that other factors that may affect the accuracy of these projections include legislation affecting federal crimes and sentencing as well as new law enforcement initiatives leading to more arrests, prosecutions, and convictions.

Table 7: BOP Projected Population, Rated Capacity, and Percentage Crowding from Fiscal Years 2012 through 2014

Security level of facility	2012			2013			2014		
	Pop	Cap	% Cro	Pop	Cap	% Cro	Pop	Cap	% Cro
Total BOP inmates	222,768			229,268			233,765		
BOP institutions	182,624	128,433	42%	188,051	131,435	43%	190,187	134,175	42%
Males	169,921	119,177	43%	174,958	120,973	45%	176,873	123,177	44%
Long-term	152,414	105,923	44%	157,353	107,719	46%	159,202	109,923	45%
Minimum	21,795	18,604	17%	22,597	18,796	20%	22,816	18,988	20%
Low	43,105	32,211	34%	44,045	32,211	37%	43,824	32,211	36%
Medium	65,993	40,583	63%	68,501	42,137	63%	69,873	43,239	62%
High	21,521	14,525	48%	22,210	14,575	52%	22,690	15,485	47%
Florence ADX[a]	441	490	-10%	444	490	-9%	444	490	-9%
Medical	2,566	2,552	1%	2,647	2,552	4%	2,704	2,552	6%
Detention	14,085	9,828	43%	14,085	9,828	43%	14,085	9,828	43%
Witness security[b]	415	384	8%	429	384	12%	438	384	14%
Females	12,703	9,256	37%	13,093	10,462	25%	13,315	10,998	21%
Long-term	11,322	8,096	40%	11,697	9,302	26%	11,909	9,838	21%
Minimum	5,285	4,264	24%	5,470	4,470	22%	5,550	4,470	24%
Secure	6,017	3,808	58%	6,207	4,808	29%	6,339	5,344	19%
High	20	24	-19%	20	24	-16%	21	24	-14%
Medical	448	378	19%	462	378	22%	472	378	25%
Detention	933	782	19%	933	782	19%	933	782	19%
Contract	40,144			41,218			43,578		
Males	38,330			39,334			41,630		
Juveniles	144			148			152		
Residential Reentry Centers	7,609			7,609			8,215		
Long-term (criminal aliens)	24,186			25,186			26,686		
Taft	2,347			2,347			2,347		
D.C. felons	0			0			0		
Jail-detention	1,783			1,783			1,783		
Home Confinement	2,261			2,261			2,448		
Females	1,814			1,883			1,948		
Juveniles	21			21			22		
Residential Reentry Centers	1,219			1,288			1,317		
Long-term	0			0			0		
D.C. felons	0			0			0		
Jail-detention	208			208			208		
Home Confinement	366			366			401		

Table 7: BOP Projected Population, Rated Capacity, and Percentage Crowding from Fiscal Years 2015 through 2017

Security level of facility	2015			2016			2017		
	Pop	Cap	% Cro	Pop	Cap	% Cro	Pop	Cap	% Cro
Total BOP inmates	237,884			242,003			246,122		
BOP institutions	192,567	134,175	44%	194,947	134,675	45%	197,327	135,175	46%
Males	179,074	123,177	45%	181,220	123,677	47%	183,366	124,177	48%
Long-term	161,344	109,923	47%	163,430	109,923	49%	165,517	109,923	51%
Minimum	23,260	18,988	22%	23,704	18,988	25%	24,149	18,988	27%
Low	43,755	32,211	36%	43,687	32,211	36%	43,619	32,211	35%
Medium	71,198	43,239	65%	72,467	43,239	68%	73,737	43,239	71%
High	23,131	15,485	49%	23,572	15,485	52%	24,012	15,485	55%
Florence ADX[a]	443	490	-9%	444	490	-9%	443	490	-10%
Medical	2,755	2,552	8%	2,806	2,552	10%	2,858	2,552	12%
Detention	14,085	9,828	43%	14,085	10,328	36%	14,085	10,828	30%
Witness security[b]	446	384	16%	454	384	18%	463	384	20%
Females	13,493	10,998	23%	13,727	10,998	25%	13,962	10,998	27%
Long-term	12,079	9,838	23%	12,304	9,838	25%	12,529	9,838	27%
Minimum	5,598	4,470	25%	5,703	4,470	28%	5,807	4,470	30%
Secure	6,459	5,344	21%	6,580	5,344	23%	6,700	5,344	25%
High	21	24	-13%	21	24	-11%	22	24	-9%
Medical	481	378	27%	490	378	30%	499	378	32%
Detention	933	782	19%	933	782	19%	933	782	19%
Contract	45,317			47,055			48,794		
Males	43,336			45,042			46,747		
Juveniles	155			157			160		
Residential Reentry Centers	8,371			8,527			8,683		
Long-term (criminal aliens)	28,186			29,686			31,186		
Taft	2,347			2,347			2,347		
D.C. felons	0			0			0		
Jail-detention	1,783			1,783			1,783		
Home Confinement	2,495			2,541			2,588		
Females	1,981			2,014			2,047		
Juveniles	22			22			23		
Residential Reentry Centers	1,342			1,367			1,392		
Long-term	0			0			0		
D.C. felons	0			0			0		
Jail-detention	208			208			208		
Home Confinement	408			416			424		

Table 7: BOP Projected Population, Rated Capacity, and Percentage Crowding from Fiscal Years 2018 through 2020

Security level of facility	2018			2019			2020		
	Pop	Cap	% Cro	Pop	Cap	% Cro	Pop	Cap	% Cro
Total BOP inmates	250,241			254,360			258,479		
BOP institutions	199,710	138,111	45%	202,088	145,871	39%	204,470	151,895	35%
Males	185,514	127,113	46%	187,659	134,873	39%	189,805	140,897	35%
Long-term	167,605	112,859	49%	169,691	120,619	41%	171,777	126,643	36%
Minimum	24,593	19,884	24%	25,037	21,932	14%	25,482	22,700	12%
Low	43,551	32,211	35%	43,482	32,211	35%	43,414	32,211	35%
Medium	75,010	43,839	71%	76,279	46,191	65%	77,549	49,047	58%
High	24,452	16,925	44%	24,893	20,285	23%	25,332	22,685	12%
Florence ADX[a]	443	490	-10%	442	490	-10%	443	490	-10%
Medical	2,909	2,552	14%	2,961	2,552	16%	3,012	2,552	18%
Detention	14,085	10,828	30%	14,085	10,828	30%	14,085	10,828	30%
Witness security[b]	471	384	23%	479	384	25%	488	384	27%
Females	14,196	10,998	29%	14,430	10,998	31%	14,665	10,998	33%
Long-term	12,755	9,838	30%	12,980	9,838	32%	13,205	9,838	34%
Minimum	5,912	4,470	32%	6,016	4,470	35%	6,121	4,470	37%
Secure	6,821	5,344	28%	6,941	5,344	30%	7,062	5,344	32%
High	22	24	-8%	23	24	-6%	23	24	-4%
Medical	508	378	34%	517	378	37%	526	378	39%
Detention	933	782	19%	933	782	19%	933	782	19%
Contract	50,533			52,272			54,010		
Males	48,453			50,159			51,864		
Juveniles	163			166			169		
Residential Reentry Centers	8,840			8,996			9,152		
Long-term (criminal aliens)	32,686			34,186			35,686		
Taft	2,347			2,347			2,347		
D.C. felons	0			0			0		
Jail-detention	1,783			1,783			1,783		
Home Confinement	2,634			2,681			2,727		
Females	2,080			2,113			2,146		
Juveniles	23			24			24		
Residential Reentry Centers	1,417			1,442			1,467		
Long-term	0			0			0		
D.C. felons	0			0			0		
Jail-detention	208			208			208		
Home Confinement	431			439			446		

Legend:

Pop refers to inmate population.

Cap refers to rated capacity of the facility.

% Cro refers to the percentage crowding.

Source: BOP.

Notes: BOP designates some of its institutions as administrative institutions, which specifically serve inmates awaiting trial, or those with intensive medical or mental health conditions, regardless of the level of supervision these inmates require.

[a]The Administrative Maximum (ADX) facility in Florence, Colorado, houses offenders requiring the tightest controls.

[b]Witness security refers to BOP housing for inmates in the federal Witness Security Program.

Assumptions:

1. The population projections for fiscal year 2012 and beyond have been adjusted.

2. BOP will activate Federal Correctional Institution Mendota, California, and Federal Correctional Institution Berlin, New Hampshire, during fiscal year 2012.

3. BOP will activate Federal Correctional Institution Hazelton, West Virginia, during fiscal year 2013.

4. BOP will activate U.S. Penitentiary Yazoo City, Mississippi, during fiscal year 2013.

5. No additional contract beds are projected to be added in fiscal year 2012.

6. One thousand additional contract beds are projected in fiscal year 2013, and 1,500 additional contract beds annually in fiscal year 2014 and beyond.

7. No increase to Residential Reentry Centers and Home Confinement is projected from fiscal years 2011 through 2013.

8. Future capacity increases are dependent upon future funding to construct new prisons and to expand the use of private prison contracts.

Appendix III: Effects of a Growing Inmate Population

This appendix presents additional information and elaboration on the effects of a growing inmate population on

- inmates,

- staff,

- infrastructure, and

- security and safety.

Inmates

The growth in the inmate population has affected inmates' daily living conditions, program participation, meaningful work opportunities, and visitation.

Daily Living

BOP uses double bunking in excess of the percentages included in a facility's rated capacity; triple bunking or converting common space (e.g., a television room) temporarily to house its growing population. BOP counts these additional beds as temporary space rather than increased rated capacity.[1] As a result of these actions to increase available bed space, more inmates are sharing cells and other living units, bringing together for longer periods of time inmates with a higher risk of violence and more potential victims.[2] Table 8 shows the temporary bed space BOP added from fiscal years 2006 through 2011 by security level and male and female facilities. During the 6-year period, the use of temporary space generally increased in male medium, and high security facilities and in female minimum security facilities, but the number of temporary beds fluctuated with changes in the number of general population beds (e.g., rated capacity).

---

[1]BOP reports the use of additional cots in areas such as an institution's halls, gyms, mezzanines, or television rooms—to address crowding in an institution—as temporary housing because (1) this temporary living space is to be restored as program space when circumstances permit and (2) the additional bathrooms and other facilities required to meet permanent housing space specifications are not added to the infrastructure. Thus, such temporary use of space is not factored into BOP's rated capacity calculation.

[2]BOP. *The Effects of Changing Crowding and Staffing Levels in Federal Prisons on Inmate Violence Rates* (Washington, D.C.: October 2005).

Table 8: Rated Capacity and Temporary Bed Space by Institutional Security Level from fiscal years 2006 through 2011

Facility type	Year											
	2006		2007		2008		2009		2010		2011	
	RC	Tem	RC	Tem	RC	Tem	RC	Tem	RC	Tem	RC	Tem
Male[a]												
Minimum	16,963	3,030	17,271	2,679	17,353	1,150	17,768	1,083	17,837	2,439	18,476	2,562
Low	31,037	11,083	30,791	9,252	31,081	9,078	32,294	11,306	32,302	10,409	32,242	10,329
Medium	37,911	10,178	39,680	12,894	38,479	13,146	39,375	14,611	40,294	13,376	41,039	16,831
High	11,528	4,367	12,428	4,781	13,448	4,830	13,430	4,678	13,570	5,252	13,570	5,472
Female[b]												
Minimum	4,429	737	4,429	862	4,429	679	4,479	521	4,479	498	4,207	853
Secure	2,800	1,947	3,394	1,811	3,394	2,081	3,994	1,540	3,808	1,707	3,808	1,902

Legend:

RC refers to rated capacity.

Tem refers to temporary bed space, not including disciplinary housing beds.

Source: GAO analysis of BOP data.

Notes: Total bed space, not including disciplinary housing beds, is the sum of RC plus Tem.

[a]Male long-term institutions include four security level designations—minimum, low, medium, and high. Female facilities include three security designations—high, secure, and minimum.

[b]Female high security facilities did not experience crowding during the 6-year period.

BOP officials told us that they were aware of the use of temporary beds in BOP's 117 institutions, but BOP does not track whether a facility uses television rooms or triple bunks in a cell. Instead, when temporary beds are added, BOP generally refers to this as triple bunking. As shown in table 9, all of the BOP facilities we visited reported using temporary beds during the period from fiscal years 2006 through 2011. At the time of our visits in 2011 and 2012, these facilities continued to use temporary space, with the exception of SeaTac.

Table 9: Rated Capacity and Temporary Bed Space of Selected BOP Facilities from Fiscal Years 2006 through 2011

	Year											
	2006		2007		2008		2009		2010		2011	
Facility[a]	RC	Tem	RC	Tem	RC	Tem	RC	Tem	RC	Tem	RC	Tem
Petersburg (low)	858	356	834	414	834	381	834	413	834	225	834	371
Petersburg (medium)	1,152	364	1,152	481	1,108	686	1,108	759	1,108	596	1,108	557
SeaTac	736	152	768	179	768	56	768	39	722	(59)	722	(71)
Lewisburg (Special Management Unit)[b]	72	(21)	72	(11)	72	25	528	237	720	281	720	429
Lewisburg (general population)	698	607	698	648	698	615	242	(40)	160	(47)	160	41
Schuylkill (medium)	720	473	848	382	848	379	848	446	848	293	848	400
Leavenworth (medium)	1,193	476	1,193	372	1,193	556	1,193	516	1,193	515	1,193	505

Legend:

RC refers to rated capacity.

Tem refers to temporary bed space, not including disciplinary housing beds.

Source: GAO analysis of BOP data.

Notes: The parentheses represent beds available above the rated capacity, but not used. The beds were available because of specific institutional changes, such as the conversion of Lewisburg to a Special Management Unit. During fiscal years 2010 and 2011, the temporary female beds at SeaTac were not used.

[a]The Petersburg, Lewisburg, Schuylkill, and Leavenworth facilities are male long-term institutions. Male long-term institutions include four security level designations—minimum, low, medium, and high. SeaTac is an administrative facility that specifically serves inmates awaiting trial, or those with intensive medical or mental health conditions, regardless of the level of supervision these inmates require.

[b]A Special Management Unit operates as a more controlled and restrictive environment for inmates whose interaction requires greater management to ensure the safety, security, or orderly operation of BOP facilities, or protection of the public. BOP established a Special Management Unit at Lewisburg Penitentiary in fiscal year 2008, and subsequently converted the entire facility to a Special Management Unit, with the exception of a unit housing general population high security inmates.

According to all of the regional directors and wardens in the two facilities we visited, different regions and facilities used different approaches to temporary bed space. For example, one regional director said that all facilities in his region used some temporary space to house inmates, but generally, institutions were no longer using television rooms to house inmates. He said that it is safer to manage 3 inmates in one cell through triple bunking than to manage 16 inmates in a converted television room.

Alternatively, at a medium security facility we visited in another region, officials told us that all inmates were double bunked in cells and the facility had converted four former television rooms to temporarily house 8 to 10 inmates in each. In each housing unit, all televisions were relocated to a single common room. BOP headquarters officials noted that having a single television room is a common cause of disciplinary incidents because fighting may erupt among groups of inmates who want to watch different programs.

In addition to crowding in a facility's housing and common areas, inmates may experience crowded bathroom facilities, reductions in shower times, shortened meal times coupled with longer waits for food service, and more limited recreational activities because of the increased inmate population. For example, with more inmates, it takes longer for correctional officers to escort inmates to the dining hall and for each inmate to be served in the food service line. According to BOP officials, extended wait times at meals in particular can be problematic because BOP attempts to keep inmates on strict schedules and extended waits may cause inmates to arrive late for vocational classes or work assignments, which can delay the start of the class or assignment. The increased inmate population also affects recreation space and activity time.[3] For example, according to staff at one BOP facility we visited, in a crowded arts room, inmates may accidentally bump elbows, resulting in tension or friction, which may lead to a security incident. At another BOP facility, with a rated capacity of 850 but housing 1,300 inmates, officials said that crowding affects accessibility to recreational activities such as team sports, especially during warmer weather, when 500 inmates may be in a recreational area supervised by one or two staff.

---

[3]Non-U.S. citizens or deportable aliens can participate in recreation programs (e.g., leisure, fitness, wellness, or sports activities). A deportable alien is an alien in the United States and admitted to the United States subject to any grounds of removal specified in the Immigration and Nationality Act, 8 U.S.C. § 1227. This includes any alien illegally in the United States, regardless of whether the alien entered the country by fraud or misrepresentation or entered legally but subsequently violated the terms of his or her nonimmigrant classification or status.

Program Participation

BOP provides programs including education, vocational training, drug treatment, and faith-based reentry programs that help to rehabilitate inmates and support correctional management.[4] According to BOP officials, two benefits of inmate programming are (1) public safety, and (2) institutional safety and security because of reduced inmate idleness. These officials said, however, that the growth in the inmate population had increased program waiting lists, contributing to inmate idleness.[5]

BOP officials said facility staff offer a variety of education programs, such as mandatory General Educational Development (GED) courses; 8- to 10-week nonmandatory courses on topics such as parenting, word processing, and conversational Spanish; occupational training; and computer-based self-paced courses (e.g., English).[6] According to BOP data, overall inmate participation in one or more programs ranged from 35 to 37 percent from fiscal years 2006 through 2011.[7] The percentage participation, number of inmates on waiting lists, and length of the average waiting time varied by program. For example, BOP snapshots from fiscal years 2008 through 2012 of the total population at BOP-run facilities showed that between 13 and 14 percent of inmates were enrolled in literacy programs, while

---

[4] See GAO-01-483.

[5] BOP also houses low security non-U.S. citizens in private contract facilities. BOP's contracts require the private providers to provide all programs (1) in accordance with the contract, which requires compliance with ACA standards and (2) as outlined in the contractors' technical proposals. According to BOP, most private contract facilities provide work and self-improvement opportunities to inmates.

[6] According to BOP, non-U.S. citizens or deportable aliens housed in BOP facilities are exempt from the required participation in the GED program, but are encouraged to attend these courses. These inmates can also participate in English as a Second Language courses, adult continuing education classes (e.g., typing and computer literacy), a release preparation program, and parenting classes. Additionally, these inmates may participate in BOP's occupational education programs if BOP resources permit after meeting the needs of other eligible inmates.

[7] BOP's Monthly Participation Reports provide a snapshot of program participation levels of inmates within BOP facilities. Figures for overall inmate participation do not duplicate. That is, if an inmate is enrolled in more than one program area (for example GED and parenting), the inmate's participation is counted only once.

between 11 and 12 percent remained on waiting lists.[8] Table 10 shows systemwide participation rates in selected BOP education and training programs as of September 2011.

Table 10: Systemwide Inmate Participation Rates in Selected BOP Programs in September 2011

	At least one program	GED classes	Adult continuing education	Occupational training	Parent education	Postsecondary programs[a]
Inmate participation rate[b]	36%	13%	11%	7%	2%	1%

Source: GAO analysis of BOP data.

[a]Post Secondary Education is a program category that is funded by inmates' personal funds rather than through BOP's salaries and expenses budget account. The curriculum extends through an associate's degree.

[b]Some programs are not offered year-round (for example parenting), and if the participation snapshot occurs when a program is not in session, the participation level will be zero.

BOP provides inmates with the opportunity to participate in a variety of drug treatment programs. In more than half of its facilities, BOP offers a residential drug abuse treatment program. In all of its facilities, BOP offers nonresidential drug abuse and drug education programs. All of the drug treatment and drug education programs had waiting lists from fiscal years 2006 through 2011. According to BOP officials, if BOP cannot meet the substance abuse treatment or education needs of inmates because it does not have the staff needed to meet program demand, some inmates will not receive programming benefits. As we reported in February 2012, long waiting lists for BOP's Residential Drug Abuse Program (RDAP), which provides sentence reductions for eligible inmates who successfully

---

[8]Enrollment figures include participation in GED classes and programs BOP is piloting but has not yet implemented on a wider scale. BOP defines the literacy wait list to include those inmates who are capable of participating and willing to participate in the literacy program and who are not enrolled in the GED program, English as a Second Language (ESL) program, or a literacy pilot program. Snapshots of the literacy program waiting lists in January and February 2012 at the facilities we visited were Petersburg medium (250), Petersburg low (93), Lewisburg (13), Schuylkill (36), Leavenworth (187), and SeaTac (78).

complete the program,[9] constrained BOP's ability to admit participants early enough to earn their maximum allowable reductions in times served.[10] From fiscal years 2009 through 2011, the number of slots for inmates to participate in RDAP increased by 400. According to BOP officials, as RDAP capacity has increased, BOP has reduced waiting lists even with continued growth in the inmate population, thereby enabling inmates to enter the program sooner and increasing the number of inmates (from 14 to 25 percent) who complete the program and receive a sentence reduction. Nevertheless, the program continues to experience long waiting lists, although the average wait has declined. For example, in low security facilities in fiscal year 2006, 3,547 inmates participated in the RDAP program, 3,378 inmates were on the waiting list, and the average waiting time was about 205 days. In contrast, in low security facilities in fiscal year 2011, 3,082 inmates participated in the program, 3,723 were on the waiting list, but the average waiting time was approximately 80 days. Tables 11-13 provide additional data on participation, waiting lists, and average waiting time for BOP drug education and treatment programs in male facilities.

---

[9]Under 28 C.F.R. § 550.53(b), to be admitted into RDAP, inmates must meet the following criteria: (1) inmates must have a verifiable substance use disorder; (2) inmates must sign an agreement acknowledging program responsibility; and (3) when beginning the program, the inmate must be able to complete all components of the program. Under 28 C.F.R. § 550.55, inmates may be eligible for early release by a period not to exceed 12 months if they meet the following criteria: (1) were sentenced to a term of imprisonment under either (i) 18 U.S.C. Chapter 227, Subchapter D for a nonviolent offense (i.e., an inmate who committed a federal offense on or after November 1, 1987, after the effective date of the Sentencing Reform Act of 1987, also known as "new law."); or (ii) D.C. Code § 24-403.01 for a nonviolent offense, meaning an offense other than those included within the definition of "crime of violence" in D.C. Code § 23-1331(4); and (2) successfully complete a RDAP during their current commitment. To receive the full-sentence reduction of 12 months, inmates are required to participate in the program for 27 months. "Old law" inmates who are parole eligible, may, at the U.S. Parole Commission's discretion, be considered for an advanced release date through an award of Superior Program Achievement.

[10]For more on RDAP, see GAO-12-320.

Table 11: BOP's Drug Education Programs in Male Facilities: Inmate Participation Levels, Waiting List Numbers, and Average Waiting Time, by Institutional Security Level from the End of Fiscal Years 2006 through 2011

Program participation by security level	Year					
	2006	2007	2008	2009	2010	2011
High						
Participation	2,578	2,394	2,378	3,716	3,195	3,198
Waiting list	2,984	3,700	3,808	6,268	5,129	4,681
Average wait in days	324.5	333.6	298.1	209.2	190.5	105.0
Medium						
Participation	9,016	9,159	9,344	11,448	14,074	12,523
Waiting list	10,436	12,193	12,467	17,948	17,474	18,231
Average wait in days	230.2	228.6	192.0	159.5	123.7	82.6
Low						
Participation	7,804	7,826	8,560	10,490	11,263	10,130
Waiting list	9,892	9,200	9,749	17,909	18,527	19,992
Average wait in days	223.4	197.7	160.4	168.7	143.1	84.4
Minimum						
Participation	4,959	4,872	4,084	5,423	5,291	5,183
Waiting list	6,269	5,857	5,124	7,104	7,043	7,400
Average wait in days	141.5	136.8	130.4	102.4	90.5	63.2
Administrative						
Participation	833	813	646	746	628	769
Waiting list	789	756	669	1,088	1,118	1,295
Average wait in days	180.5	150.7	153.2	130.9	111.2	73.7

Source: GAO analysis of BOP data.

Note: Drug education programs are distinct from residential and nonresidential drug treatment programs.

Table 12: BOP's Nonresidential Drug Treatment Programs in Male Facilities: Inmate Participation Levels, Waiting List Numbers, and Average Waiting Time, by Institutional Security Level from the End of Fiscal Years 2006 through 2011

Program participation by security level	Year					
	2006	2007	2008	2009	2010	2011
High						
Participation	493	585	554	818	566	946
Waiting list	160	197	397	465	699	1,388
Average wait in days	253.4	264.7	310.4	395.0	199.1	101.3
Medium						
Participation	2,480	3,281	4,195	3,411	3,446	4,852
Waiting list	568	774	997	2,723	3,688	4,707
Average wait in days	299.2	266.1	214.1	204.4	178.0	98.5
Low						
Participation	4,088	4,747	4,127	3,717	3,538	4,931
Waiting list	1,070	1,615	1,704	2,691	3,570	3,842
Average wait in days	160.9	184.4	188.2	211.4	169.9	79.8
Minimum						
Participation	2,475	2,820	2,559	3,040	3,055	3,984
Waiting list	596	676	980	1,989	2,531	3,115
Average wait in days	223.0	217.5	165.8	171.7	151.4	85.3
Administrative						
Participation	224	239	247	218	195	759
Waiting list	111	184	172	202	200	523
Average wait in days	121.8	268.0	244.3	226.2	125.6	59.3

Source: GAO analysis of BOP data.

Table 13: BOP's Residential Drug Abuse Programs in Male Facilities: Inmate Participation Levels, Waiting List Numbers, and Average Waiting Time, by Institutional Security Level from the End of Fiscal Years 2006 through 2011

Program participation by security level	Year					
	2006	2007	2008	2009	2010	2011
High[a]						
Participation	63	1	0	2	0	0
Waiting list	354	298	305	277	226	245
Average wait in days	377.0	322.5	324.9	292.8	231.3	131.1
Medium						
Participation	1,772	1,884	2,008	2,114	2,220	2,379
Waiting list	2,577	2,770	3,054	2,745	2,546	2,928
Average wait in days	242.3	226.5	213.6	194.8	147.1	92.8
Low						
Participation	3,547	3,326	3,256	2,987	3,398	3,082
Waiting list	3,378	3,409	3,773	3,185	3,264	3,723
Average wait in days	205.3	174.6	178.0	166.2	125.3	80.2
Minimum						
Participation	3,704	3,443	3,789	3,764	3,719	3,231
Waiting list	4,104	3,931	3,998	3,440	3,379	3,758
Average wait in days	258.8	237.6	223.9	202.9	145.6	83.8
Administrative						
Participation	64	31	92	56	75	65
Waiting list	145	87	149	108	92	106
Average wait in days	279.6	224.2	199.8	187.7	156.6	87.1

Source: GAO analysis of BOP data.

[a]According to BOP officials, high security facilities currently do not offer a Residential Drug Abuse Program, but because the program is offered near an inmate's release date, high security inmates may apply for the program and may be able transfer to a lower security level facility that offers the program by the time they are ready for release. BOP plans to activate Residential Drug Abuse Programs in high security facilities in fiscal year 2013 and has requested funding for this program in its fiscal year 2013 budget submission.

BOP also implements two faith-based reentry programs through its Religious Services Branch. Life Connections is BOP's 18-month residential program, begun in 2002, that offers a core curriculum taught by spiritual guides hired from different faiths. The number of enrollments in the program ranged from 345 to almost 400 inmates systemwide. The program waiting lists for each security level were generally equal to or greater than the number of participants. Threshold is BOP's nonresidential faith-based program, which began in 2008. Over 550 inmates were enrolled in the program as of January 2012; maintaining a

waiting list for Threshold program participation is at the discretion of
participating institutions' wardens.

*Meaningful Work
Opportunities*

According to BOP headquarters officials, the growth in the federal inmate
population has also affected inmate work opportunities, as it is difficult to
find meaningful work for all inmates in a crowded facility, even though
generally all inmates are required to have a job.[11] They said that with the
growth of the prison population, fewer opportunities exist to engage in
meaningful work. This makes it difficult for staff to keep inmates busy,
resulting in inmate idleness, which can lead to additional tension and
fighting between inmates. Inmate discord can then affect the security and
safety of other inmates and staff. For example, BOP headquarters
officials and the warden at one facility we visited explained that inmate
wages vary with the job. Specifically, wages may range from 12 cents per
hour for sweeping the facility to $1.15 per hour for some jobs in factories
that Federal Prison Industries, also known as UNICOR, runs on the
prison grounds. Tensions may arise because inmates want to be
reassigned from lower- to higher-paying jobs. According to BOP officials,
BOP has tried to develop an index of idleness; however, measuring
idleness is difficult because inmates are usually engaged in some activity,
even though that activity may not be meaningful to their development
(e.g., filling salt shakers in the cafeteria).

Facility officials underscored that the most desirable jobs in the facilities
were those in UNICOR factories.[12] These factories (1) produce items
such as furniture, office supplies, and uniforms for sale to government
customers and (2) perform services for both government and private
sector purchase. Officials at one medium security facility we visited told

---

[11] The Crime Control Act of 1990, Pub. L. No. 101-647, § 2905, 104 Stat. 4789, 4914
(codified at 18 U.S.C. § 4121 note) established a mandatory work requirement for all
prisoners. Specifically, this section provided that in general, it is the policy of the federal
government that convicted inmates confined in federal prisons, jails, and other detention
facilities shall work. The type of work in which they will be involved shall be dictated by
appropriate security considerations and by the health of the prisoner involved. A federal
prisoner may be excused from the requirement to work only as necessitated by security
considerations; disciplinary action; medical certification of disability such as would make it
impracticable for prison officials to arrange useful work for the prisoner to perform; or a
need for the prisoner to work less than a full work schedule in order to participate in
literacy training, drug rehabilitation, or similar programs in addition to the work program.

[12] Non-U.S. citizens who are currently under an order of deportation, exclusion, or
removal from the United States are precluded from participating in the UNICOR program,
under 28 C.F.R. § 345.35.

us that these jobs teach inmates valuable reentry skills, such as coming to work on time.[13] Such jobs can also teach money management and budgeting, and because the earnings are higher than those for other prison jobs, inmates have the opportunity to send money home to their families. As a result, officials said there is less idleness among inmates with UNICOR jobs, which helps to support security and safety in the facility, and that the recidivism rate for participants is lower.[14] Facility officials also noted that the decline in the number of UNICOR jobs has resulted in waiting lists and challenged staff to create jobs to support industrial work programming. Systemwide, the number of UNICOR factories peaked at 110 in 2007, declining to 88 in 2011. These factories employed over 23,000 inmates in 2007, declining to 14,200 inmates in 2011. In May 2010 the waiting list for UNICOR jobs was over 26,000 inmates, with an average waiting time of 16 months.[15] According to BOP officials, a UNICOR waiting list includes inmates from the facility where the factory is located. An inmate transferring to a facility may be placed on the waiting list, but an inmate cannot be transferred to a facility to participate in the UNICOR program. At one facility we visited, officials told us that approximately 200 inmates were on the waiting list. They explained that the waiting list consisted of three groups: inmates with financial responsibilities, inmates with prior UNICOR experience, and inmates on the general waiting list. When slots opened up, inmates were selected equally from each of the three lists.

---

[13] Reentry refers to the transition of inmates from prisons or jails back into the community. It is BOP's philosophy that preparation for reentry begins on the first day of an inmate's incarceration.

[14] William G. Saylor and Gerald G. Gaes. *PREP: Training Inmates through Industrial Work Participation, and Vocational and Apprenticeship Instruction,* Federal Bureau of Prisons (Washington, D.C.: Sept. 24, 1996), and Saylor and Gaes. *The Differential Effect of Industries and Vocational Training on Post Release Outcome for Ethnic and Racial Groups,* Federal Bureau of Prisons (Washington, D.C.: Sept. 8, 1999). Recidivism generally refers to a former inmate's relapse into criminal behavior, and although agencies may measure recidivism in different manners, recidivism measures can include the rearrest, reconviction, or re-incarceration of former inmates.

[15] The waiting lists by security level were minimum (638), low (2,549), medium (13,154), high (9,439), and maximum (569). The source for these data is Marketing Research & Corporate Support.

Visitation

Crowded visiting rooms make it more difficult for inmates to visit with their families. BOP headquarters officials said the quality of the interaction between an inmate and family can positively affect an inmate's behavior in prison and aids an inmate's success when returning to the community. Each BOP facility has visiting space to accommodate the number of inmates that the facility was designed to house and a visitor capacity to enable staff to manage the visitation process. The infrastructure of the facility may not support the increase in visitors as a result of the growth in the prison population. Further, with more inmates, the visitation process requires more staff resources. BOP officials explained that the visiting process requires at least four staff—one in the front lobby to process visitors, one to escort inmates in and out of the visiting room and search the inmate for contraband following the visit, one to document and search visitors to prevent the introduction of contraband, and one to walk around the visiting area supervising interactions.

Limited visiting capacity and the larger numbers of inmates can lead to frustrations for inmates and visitors, such as when visits are shorter or visitors are turned away because there are too many visitors on a particular day. Five of the regional directors and officials at four of the facilities we visited reported that the effect of the population growth on visitation varied by region and facilities within the region because of a number of factors, including proximity of the facility to inmates' families. If a large percentage of the inmate population is from the area where the facility is located, the visiting room is used at a greater frequency. Conversely, if inmates' families do not live near the facility, the increase in the number of inmates does not have a similar effect on visitation. For example, one regional director told us that the increase in the number of inmates had not affected overall visitation in the region because of the large number of inmates who were non-U.S. citizens and whose families did not visit. In another region, the regional director told us that some facilities have problems with visitation only on holidays, when families wish to be together, while others have problems regularly. According to officials, allowing all inmates rather than none or some inmates to have visitors helps inmates' morale and facility management.

Additionally, the larger number of inmates also limits inmate access to the telephone to call home and computer to e-mail family members and other contacts.[16] For example, at one facility we visited, each housing unit had three telephones for about 156 inmates. We reported in September 2011 that BOP provided a variety of options to its inmates for making phone calls to friends and families; nevertheless, the number of contraband cell phones in prisons had risen. Given the potential that these phones provide for furthering criminal activity (e.g., selling drugs), the illicit use of cell phones can pose a danger to staff and inmates, as well as the public at large.[17]

Correctional Staff

Facility officials told us that because of the large prison population, correctional officers do not have time to use their interpersonal correctional skills and maintain communication between staff and individual inmates. Representatives of the correctional workers' union and officials at three of the five prisons we visited specifically emphasized the importance of interaction and communication between inmates and correctional staff for purposes of inmate reentry and facility management. During one site visit, we observed that facility department heads and unit managers stand along the cafeteria serving line during meals to provide the opportunity for inmates to speak with staff about problems and concerns.[18] A union representative observed that inmates used to tell correctional staff about problems (e.g., where other inmates were storing contraband), but with more than one inmate in a cell, inmates may not want to talk to the correctional officer in front of the other inmates.

Tables 14 through 16 provide historical data on inmate to total BOP staff ratios, inmate to BOP institutional staff ratios, and inmate to BOP correctional staff ratios.

---

[16]Through BOP's system for e-mail, inmates can communicate with a list of contacts, but they cannot access the Internet. Both inmates and persons in the community with whom they correspond must consent to having all incoming and outgoing electronic messages monitored and retained by BOP staff.

[17]GAO, *Bureau of Prisons: Improved Evaluations and Increased Coordination Could Improve Cell Phone Detection*, GAO-11-893 (Washington, D.C.: Sept. 6, 2011).

[18]According to BOP, this practice also affords security additional to that provided by uniformed correctional officers, as these administrators and staff are also trained correctional officers.

Table 14: BOP Inmate to Total BOP Staff Ratios from Fiscal Years 1997 through 2011

Year	Total S&E staff onboard	BOP institution population	Inmate to staff ratio by fiscal year
1997	28,302	101,091	3.57
1998	28,870	108,207	3.75
1999	29,176	117,295	4.02
2000	30,382	125,560	4.13
2001	31,806	130,327	4.10
2002	31,823	137,527	4.32
2003	32,265	146,212	4.53
2004	32,746	152,518	4.66
2005	32,735	159,501	4.87
2006	33,114	162,514	4.91
2007	33,994	167,323	4.92
2008	34,139	165,964	4.86
2009	34,914	172,423	4.94
2010	35,972	173,289	4.82
2011	35,987	177,934	4.94

Source: BOP data.

Note: The President's annual budget justification to Congress for BOP includes a systemwide inmate to total BOP staff ratio. This ratio is systemwide rather than by facility security level. BOP calculates this ratio using (1) the inmate population at each facility on the last day of the fiscal year and (2) the total number of BOP staff on board as of the last pay period of the fiscal year. The total number of BOP staff includes all staff at BOP institutions, regional offices, training centers, and the central office (i.e., staff funded by BOP's Salaries & Expenses (S&E) appropriation and Public Health Service (PHS) staff).

Table15: BOP's Inmate to Total Institutional Staff Ratios from Fiscal Years 2006 through 2011

	2006	2007	2008	2009	2010	2011
Systemwide	5.2	5.2	5.2	5.2	5.2	5.2
Administrative	6	5.7	5.5	5.1	5	4.9
Complex	5.1	5.4	5.4	5.3	5.1	5.3
Detention	4.6	4.4	4.6	4.6	4.5	4.6
High	4.5	4.5	4.2	4.1	4.1	4.1
Low	6.6	6.1	6	6.1	6.2	6.1
Medical	3	2.7	2.8	2.9	2.8	2.8
Medium	5.4	5.5	5.6	5.5	5.5	5.6
Minimum	8	8	7.6	7.6	7.6	8
Female facilities	5.7	5.7	5.7	5.5	5.2	5.2
Male facilities	5.2	5.2	5.2	5.2	5.2	5.2

Source: GAO analysis of BOP data.

Note: For purposes of this table, a ratio of "x:1" is expressed more simply as "x." These ratios were calculated using the following information. The inmate population used to calculate the ratio is based on the Fiscal Year Average Daily Population (ADP) for each facility. ADP is calculated by totaling the total inmate days recorded at each facility for the fiscal year and dividing that number by the number of days in the fiscal year. The staffing level used to calculate the ratio is based on the fiscal year end onboard staffing level at each facility as of the last pay period of the fiscal year. S&E and PHS staff onboard at year end were included in this calculation. The calculation excludes Buildings and Facilities, UNICOR, and Trust Fund staff as well as all staff at regional offices, training centers, and central office locations and facilities that were in the activation process.

Table 16: Snapshots of BOP's Inmate to Correctional Officer Ratios, by BOP Region, from Fiscal Years 2006 through 2011

Region	Ratios	2006	2007	2008	2009	2010	2011
Mid-Atlantic	Low ratio	7.8	3.6	8.1	7.4	7.9	7.5
	High ratio	24.4	26	23.3	22.5	24.6	25.3
	Average ratio	11.5	10.5	11	10.8	10.3	10.6
North Central	Low ratio	1.6	4.9	5.2	5.3	5.0	5.3
	High ratio	37	26	25.8	28.2	26.7	28.6
	Average ratio	9	8.8	9.1	9.3	8.8	9.3
Northeast	Low ratio	6.9	5.5	4.6	5.9	5.5	5.9
	High ratio	21.7	17.2	17.8	24.6	19.8	14.6
	Average ratio	11.8	10.4	10.3	10.6	10.3	10.1
South Central	Low ratio	7.6	7.5	6.7	7.1	7.3	7.8
	High ratio	31.7	29.6	24.2	24.1	22.3	24.4
	Average ratio	13.2	12.9	11.7	12.5	12.5	12.7
Southeast	Low ratio	9.3	9.4	8.4	9.7	9.2	9.9
	High ratio	34.9	28.1	26.2	27.4	25.6	30.4
	Average ratio	12.4	12	11.8	11.8	11.6	12.2
Western	Low ratio	5.9	4.7	5.9	6.5	5.4	5.9
	High ratio	16.5	18.1	17	17.8	14.6	16.5
	Average ratio	10.4	10	9.7	9.7	9.4	10.3

Source: GAO analysis of BOP data.

Note: Correctional officer refers to those BOP staff who enforce the regulations governing the operation of a correctional institution. All values imply an inmate to correctional officer ratio of "x:1." For purposes of this table, we have omitted the "1" from the ratio and just reported the "x." BOP includes facilities not yet fully activated in its data. Thus, where a facility had an inmate-to-staff ratio of some number less than 1:1, we omitted that facility from our analysis of the high, low, and average ratios for the respective region. For example, in fiscal year 2010 and 2011, BOP listed a facility called Mendota in its listing for the Western Region. In fiscal year 2010, BOP recorded the inmate to correctional officer ratio for Mendota as 00:1 and in fiscal year 2011, BOP reported the ratio as 0.6:1. This facility was not fully activated in either year, so we omitted it from our table.

Infrastructure

Systemwide, water costs were over $25 million in fiscal year 2005 and more than $37 million in fiscal year 2011, an increase of about 48 percent. Water usage increased from 7.9 billion gallons in 2005 to 9.9 billion gallons in 2011.

More inmates results in greater water usage for heating, laundry, showers, toilets, sanitation, and food service. As a result, BOP is the largest energy and water consumer in DOJ. Specifically, BOP estimated that each inmate uses approximately 150 gallons of water per day. BOP's electricity costs also increased about 35 percent, from about $79 million in fiscal year 2005 to more than $107 million in fiscal year 2011. According to BOP, the main reason for this increase is the rising cost of electricity over the last 6 years, although more inmates with more laundry also have had a marginal impact. BOP regional and facility officials said that with the increased population, the food service equipment is used to prepare more meals, thereby shortening the life of the equipment.

In February 2012, BOP reported 150 major unfunded repair projects (i.e., each project had an estimated repair cost of $300,000 or more) for a total projected repair cost of almost $346 million. These included unfunded repairs totaling about $30 million for four of the five prisons we visited, such as replacement of a roof, repairs to the perimeter wall, replacement of the perimeter fence, and upgrading a sewer system. One regional director observed, however, that when BOP does not have funding for repairs, staff find a way to "make do." For example, at one older facility in that region, staff built a second roof over the computer room, rather than undertake the more costly roof repair, because the main roof of the facility leaked.

BOP officials said facilities are so crowded that closing older facilities is not an option. These officials explained that BOP's goal is to reduce crowding to 15 percent systemwide. Because BOP projects continued population growth and does not anticipate a large increase in facility capacity, a significant decrease in the population would have to occur before BOP would be able to consider facility closures. Officials said that before closing BOP-run facilities, BOP would reduce its private prison contracts, but reductions in facility space would also depend on the security level of the population where reductions occurred.

Security and Safety

According to BOP officials, the increasing inmate population and staffing ratios negatively affect inmate conduct and the imposition of discipline, thereby affecting security and safety. BOP maintains an inmate discipline program for all inmates in BOP custody, which is to help ensure the safety, security, and orderly operation of correctional facilities, as well as the protection of the public, by allowing BOP staff to impose sanctions on inmates who commit prohibited acts.[19] BOP classifies prohibited acts into four levels according to the severity of the offense and provides a range of sanctions.[20] Available sanctions are based on the severity of the offense and include disallowance and forfeiture of good conduct time credit, disciplinary segregation, loss of privileges (e.g., visitation, telephone, and commissary).[21] BOP disciplinary hearing data show an increase from fiscal years 2006 through 2010 and a decline in fiscal year 2011.[22] Table 17 shows the trends in the number of guilty findings for each level of prohibited acts from fiscal years 2006 through 2011. According to BOP officials, moderate severity (300-level) prohibited acts include less serious but more frequently committed types of inmate misconduct, such as insolent behavior toward staff, thus explaining the large number of findings reported for this category.

[19] BOP's inmate discipline program is authorized by 18 U.S.C. § 4042(a)(3).

[20] BOP has four levels of offenses, ranging from level 100 to level 400: greatest severity level (100) offenses (e.g., killing, serious assault, and possession of weapons), high severity level (200) offenses (e.g., fighting or threatening bodily harm), moderate severity level (300) offenses (e.g., being in an unauthorized area, refusing an order, or insolence), and low severity level (400) offenses (e.g., feigning illness).

[21] Generally, BOP is authorized to award up to 54 days of good conduct time credit for each year served (which vests on the date the inmate is released). Good conduct time credit may be awarded to an inmate serving a sentence of more than 1 year, but less than life. The credit may be disallowed for an inmate found to have committed a prohibited act. Loss of good conduct time credit is a mandatory disciplinary sanction for Violent Crime Control and Law Enforcement Act of 1994 violent inmates, Prison Reform Litigation Act inmates, and D.C. Code offenders pursuant to 28 C.F.R. § 541.4. The amount of good conduct time disallowed is based upon the severity level of the offense and is a sanction that may only be imposed by the disciplinary hearing officer (DHO). The DHO may also sanction an inmate to forfeiture of good conduct time, if available, as good conduct time does not vest until the inmate is released.

[22] BOP has two types of disciplinary hearings. One is conducted by the Unit Discipline Committee (UDC), which consists of two or more institution staff. The other type of hearing is conducted by the DHO, who works for the regional director. Initially, the UDC reviews the incident report. Depending on the severity of the prohibited act, the UDC may make a finding that the inmate did or did not commit the prohibited act or the UDC may refer the report to the DHO for a hearing. The DHO must make a final disposition on all greatest (100) and high (200) severity level offenses. The total number of UDC hearings increased from about 67,000 in fiscal year 2006 to about 72,700 in fiscal year 2010, declining to about 70,800 in fiscal year 2011. The total number of DHO hearings increased from about 53,000 in fiscal year 2006 to over 60,600 in fiscal year 2010 and then declined to about 59,600 in fiscal year 2011.

Table 17: Guilty Findings for Prohibited Acts by Severity Level, Fiscal Years 2006 through 2011

Fiscal years	Guilty findings for 100-level prohibited acts	Guilty findings for 200-level prohibited acts	Guilty findings for 300-level prohibited acts	Guilty findings for 400-level prohibited acts
2006	7,711	23,731	54,219	1,929
2007	8,361	24,112	51,519	2,025
2008	9,552	24,980	50,633	1,933
2009	11,021	27,386	54,043	2,125
2010	10,677	28,915	59,462	2,042
2011	10,195	27,168	60,269	1,731

Source: GAO analysis of BOP data.

Note: This table reflects only the most serious prohibited act for each incident report. One hundred-level prohibited acts are of the greatest severity (e.g., killing or assaulting a person) and 400-level acts are of the lowest severity (e.g., feigning illness).

During the 6-year period, BOP data indicated that the most frequently imposed sanctions for guilty findings were loss of privileges, disallowance of good time credit, and segregation.

In addition to maintaining individual discipline, BOP facility management may lock down a facility—a temporary situation in which all inmates are confined to their living quarters/cells until staff are able to assess the situation following a critical incident (e.g., a, assaults on staff by several inmates, or a food or work strike) and can safely return the institution to normal operations. According to BOP data, BOP systemwide imposed almost 4,000 lockdowns from fiscal years 2006 through 2011. Similar to the inmate misconduct data, the number of lockdowns increased from fiscal years 2006 through 2009, peaking at 1,042 that year and then declining to 824 in fiscal year 2011.

Appendix IV: GAO Contact and Staff Acknowledgments

GAO Contact	David C. Maurer, (202) 512-9627 or maurerd@gao.gov
Staff Acknowledgments	In addition to the contact named above, Joy Booth, Assistant Director; Pedro Almoguera; Willie Commons; Eric Hauswirth; Lara Miklozek; Linda Miller; Meghan Squires; Barbara Stolz; and Greg Wilmoth made key contributions to this report.

Related GAO Products

Federal Bureau of Prisons: Methods for Estimating Incarceration and Community Corrections Costs and Results of the Elderly Offender Pilot. GAO-12-807R. Washington, D.C.: July 27, 2012.

Bureau of Prisons: Eligibility and Capacity Impact Use of Flexibilities to Reduce Inmates' Time in Prison. GAO-12-320. Washington, D.C. February 7, 2012.

Bureau of Prisons: Improved Evaluations and Increased Coordination Could Improve Cell Phone Detection. GAO-11-893. Washington, D.C.: September 6, 2011.

Bureau of Prisons: Evaluating the Impact of Protective Equipment Could Help Enhance Officer Safety. GAO-11-410. Washington, D.C.: April 8, 2011.

Bureau of Prisons: Methods for Cost Estimation Largely Reflect Best Practices, but Quantifying Risks Would Enhance Decision Making. GAO-10-94. Washington, D.C.: November 10, 2009.

Prison Construction: Clear Communication on the Accuracy of Cost Estimates and Project Changes is Needed. GAO-08-634. Washington, D.C.: May 29, 2008.

Cost of Prisons: Bureau of Prisons Needs Better Data to Assess Alternatives for Acquiring Low and Minimum Security Facilities. GAO-08-6. Washington, D.C.: October 5, 2007.

Prisoner Releases: Trends and Information on Reintegration Programs. GAO-01-483. Washington, D.C. June 18, 2001.

State and Federal Prisoners: Profiles of Inmate Characteristics in 1991 and 1997. GAO/GGD-00-117. Washington, D.C.: May 24, 2000.

GAO's Mission	The Government Accountability Office, the audit, evaluation, and investigative arm of Congress, exists to support Congress in meeting its constitutional responsibilities and to help improve the performance and accountability of the federal government for the American people. GAO examines the use of public funds; evaluates federal programs and policies; and provides analyses, recommendations, and other assistance to help Congress make informed oversight, policy, and funding decisions. GAO's commitment to good government is reflected in its core values of accountability, integrity, and reliability.
Obtaining Copies of GAO Reports and Testimony	The fastest and easiest way to obtain copies of GAO documents at no cost is through GAO's website (http://www.gao.gov). Each weekday afternoon, GAO posts on its website newly released reports, testimony, and correspondence. To have GAO e-mail you a list of newly posted products, go to http://www.gao.gov and select "E-mail Updates."
Order by Phone	The price of each GAO publication reflects GAO's actual cost of production and distribution and depends on the number of pages in the publication and whether the publication is printed in color or black and white. Pricing and ordering information is posted on GAO's website, http://www.gao.gov/ordering.htm. Place orders by calling (202) 512-6000, toll free (866) 801-7077, or TDD (202) 512-2537. Orders may be paid for using American Express, Discover Card, MasterCard, Visa, check, or money order. Call for additional information.
Connect with GAO	Connect with GAO on Facebook, Flickr, Twitter, and YouTube. Subscribe to our RSS Feeds or E-mail Updates. Listen to our Podcasts. Visit GAO on the web at www.gao.gov.
To Report Fraud, Waste, and Abuse in Federal Programs	Contact: Website: http://www.gao.gov/fraudnet/fraudnet.htm E-mail: fraudnet@gao.gov Automated answering system: (800) 424-5454 or (202) 512-7470
Congressional Relations	Katherine Siggerud, Managing Director, siggerudk@gao.gov, (202) 512-4400, U.S. Government Accountability Office, 441 G Street NW, Room 7125, Washington, DC 20548
Public Affairs	Chuck Young, Managing Director, youngc1@gao.gov, (202) 512-4800 U.S. Government Accountability Office, 441 G Street NW, Room 7149 Washington, DC 20548